Cissy Patterson

Cissy Patterson

ALICE ALBRIGHT HOGE

RANDOM HOUSE   NEW YORK

TO MOTHER

AND

AUNT ALICIA

ACKNOWLEDGMENTS

My great aunt, Eleanor Medill Patterson, was a controversial personality and readers might be curious why a member of the family should write her biography. The answer is that "Aunt Cissy" was the legend of my childhood, and simple curiosity has provoked me to find out why. Aunt Cissy herself always liked a good story, and hers is an enthralling one.

A number of people have been generous to me in the course of this project, and now I know what it means to say that thanks cannot be expressed adequately. James F. Hoge, Jr., my husband and a newspaper editor, collaborated extensively in the organizing and writing of this book.

Among members of the family I am especially grateful to Mrs. Felicia Gizycka Magruder, Mrs. A. H. Patterson, Mrs. Josephine Patterson Albright, Ivan Albright, the late Mrs. Alicia Patterson Guggenheim, and Joseph Patterson Albright. Grateful thanks also to Mrs. Maryland Hooper McCormick, Captain Harry Guggenheim, Mrs. Mary King Patterson, Mr. and Mrs. Drew Pearson, Mrs. Ellen Pearson Arnold, and Tyler Abell.

For assorted assistances I am indebted to George Abell, Mr. and Mrs. Emil Bouchard, George Bruce Brooks, Mrs. Katherine Burt, Mrs. Gwedolyn deS. Cafritz, Mrs. Rose Crabtree, Alfred Friendly, Mrs. Alice Roosevelt Longworth, Mrs. Agnes Meyer, Edward T. Folliard, Mr. and Mrs. Arthur Krock, Mrs. Eve Robert, Mrs. Anne Bowie Smith, Miss Carolyn Hagner Shaw, William C. Shelton, Miss Adela Rogers St. John, and Mrs. Page Huidecooper Wilson.

Acknowledgments

I should like also to thank George Abbott, Miss Margaret Barney, George Backer, Dr. Alvan Barach, William Campbell, Ernest Cuneo, George Dixon, Sidney Epstein, Miss Maria C. Escandon, Mrs. Marshall Field, Miss Dorothy J. Holdsworth, Mrs. Doris Fleeson Kimball, Archie Lye, Mrs. Jules Lederer, Mrs. George T. Langhorne, Lester Markel, Mrs. Charles Grimes, Willis D. Nance, Perry Patterson, the late Honorable Adlai E. Stevenson, Mrs. Frank Allen West, Thomas J. White, Jr., and Walter Wood.

Grateful acknowledgment is given for the help given by *Newsday,* the *New York Daily News,* the *Chicago Tribune,* the Washington Club, the Bateman School of Chicago, the Library of Congress, the Washington Public Library, the Franklin D. Roosevelt Memorial Library, the Widener Library, the Chicago Historical Society, the Newberry Library, and the District court in Washington.

I am particularly indebted to Frank C. Waldrop for the spirit in which he gave me the key to two rooms of hitherto confidential files and went on a vacation.

In addition to the many histories, biographies, diaries, newspaper files, magazine articles and court files which are public record, I consulted several special sources. These include the papers of Frank Waldrop; family papers from the estate of Alicia Patterson Guggenheim; manuscripts and correspondence loaned by Felicia Gizycka Magruder; family papers and photographs loaned by Alice Higinbotham Patterson; family scrapbooks loaned by Mrs. Ivan Albright; memoranda pertaining to the will of Eleanor Patterson prepared by George Bruce Brooks of Jackson, Brophy & Brooks, New York; correspondence belonging to the estate of Colonel Robert R. McCormick; a report on the business operation of the *Washington Times Herald* prepared by William C. Shelton; and an honors thesis written for the history department of Williams College by Joseph P. Albright entitled *Joseph Medill Patterson, Right or Wrong, American;* and Frank Waldrop's manuscript of *McCormick of Chicago,* which is scheduled for publication in February, 1966.

CONTENTS

INTRODUCTION

"Cissy" was more than a nickname for Eleanor Patterson; it was a trademark and the only name she kept consistently throughout her life, from 1881 until 1948. Christened Elinor Josephine, she opted in favor of Eleanor Medill for reasons of taste and future influence when she was still a child. Her names were successively Countess Eleanora Gizycka, as the wife of a Polish aristocrat; Mrs. Schlesinger, as the wife of a Wall Street financier; and finally, Mrs. Patterson, Washington editor and publisher.

Her personality was as varied as her names. Arthur Brisbane, Cissy's journalistic father-confessor, described one facet by calling her "The Bird of Paradise." Adela Rogers St. John, the writer, thought of Cissy as the reincarnation of Elizabeth the Great, the red-haired English queen. But Cissy spoke of herself as "just a plain old vindictive shanty Irish bitch." Her consistent characteristic was her enormous physical presence, which transformed ordinary rooms into spotlighted stages.

The extravagance of her plumage suited a paradisiacal creature. Her hair was as red as fall leaves, her skin was white, and she wore sensuous, theatrical clothes to emphasize her slenderness. She wasn't beautiful, especially by the classical standards of her day. She was what the French call "belle laide." Her best assets were her voice, which was deep like a man's and very soft, and her carriage, graceful as a cat's.

And Cissy paraded through life like a queen. She lived in royal style, surrounded by a retinue, oblivious to the rules and customs which bound ordinary people. As an editor and publisher of the largest circulation newspaper in the nation's capitol she had power and she was not shy about using it. At a time when few women, especially from her background, entered the male world of business and politics Cissy used the feminine arts as a ladder to high places of influence. She learned "to handle" men, whether they were reporters, advertising prospects or inflated politicians. She was a gifted hostess, unusually well-read on public affairs, zestfully opinionated, yet—it was her charm—a good listener.

When Cissy could not catch flies with honey, she lost her temper and pulled out their wings. She was, as she said, a bitch—not like the caricature of the modern female executive, but feline in her cunning. She could over-indulge friends and then, with the flick of a mood, reject them. She plotted fine Italian schemes to express her displeasures, and too often pilloried politicians and public officials needlessly in her newspaper.

Through it all she remained Cissy, a nursery diminutive of sister and a particularly apt nickname. In big and little ways Cissy remained an adoring little sister who followed her headstrong brother, Captain Joseph Medill Patterson, founder and moving spirit of the *New York Daily News*.

With her brother Joe and her cousin, Colonel Robert McCormick of the *Chicago Tribune*, Cissy conducted a bitter campaign to keep the United States out of World War II. And after Pearl Harbor forced an interlude in the isolationist-interventionist controversy, Cissy maintained unremitting hostility to President Roosevelt and his advisors, whom she believed guilty of ordering the events that drove America to war.

From the time of Woodrow Wilson, "The Three Furies," as she and her brother and cousin were known in the 1940s, consistently opposed American commitments abroad. The nature of their opposition and its influence remain valuable subjects to study for a nation which is still testing and debating its proper role and limitations as a world power.

The passage of time has dissipated some of the emotionalism which complicated the painful birth of America as a world power. At the time, the Three Furies were certainly too quick in attributing conspiratorial motives to their political opponents. But in turn, Roosevelt and his supporters too readily dismissed the Pattersons and McCormicks as misanthropic know-nothings. History may be proving wrong the *Tribune* family's opposition to such multinational peace efforts as the League of Nations and the United Nations. But history seems to vindicate their belief that Wilson's idealistic, non-pragmatic approach to foreign affairs was not the whole answer. And their insistence on the value of military preparedness would now seem an undisputed fact in a nation which has learned the role of armed might in the preservation of peace.

Cissy, as a human being and as a journalist, was unique. She had so many assets that only her liabilities matched them. Flavored by genius and madness, as barbaric as she was exquisite, she was of the consistency of feathers and the strength of absinthe—"no glass of milk," as one of her reporters put it.

Alice Albright Hoge
Washington, D.C., 1963
Chicago, 1965

Cissy Patterson

1

Chicago Childhood

There was a saying among the women in Cissy's family: "I am rich, young, beautiful and a Medill!" It was a statement of an attitude which characterized the descendants of Joseph Medill, a strong-minded Scotch-Irishman who was Cissy's maternal grandfather.

Medill, tall and angular with black eyes and high cheekbones, was one of the founding patriarchs of the American Midwest. A contemporary of Abraham Lincoln, he too educated himself with borrowed books, put himself through law school, emigrated west to Illinois, and became active in the political movement which culminated in the founding of the Republican Party. Medill made his fortune as the editor and publisher of *The Chicago Daily Tribune,* which he eventually bought with money borrowed from Marshall Field, Chicago's most successful drygoods merchant. Along with Horace Greeley and Charles Dana, Medill was called a great American editor. His newspaper's support of Abraham Lincoln for the Republican nomination in 1860 played a role which such historians as Carl Sandburg and Frederick Bancroft acknowledge as major. In the Chicago of Medill's day newspaper editors and publishers did more than comment on politics. In 1864, for example, "Long John" Wentworth and Cyrus Hall McCormick, both publishers, were the candidates for mayor, and Joseph Medill accused them both of using their newspapers for political gain. Then, after the Great Chicago Fire in 1871, Medill himself ran for mayor and won.

Joseph Medill was not the first journalist among Cissy's ancestors. The first of them in America was James Patrick, who emigrated in 1803 to the frontier of eastern Ohio from Belfast and there became a county judge, Indian agent and land commissioner before he founded a Whig weekly called the *Tuscarawas Chronicle*. Judge Patrick gave young Joseph Medill his first newspaper job and the hand of his daughter, Catherine, a redhead.

The three daughters of Joseph and Catherine Medill were tall, red-headed, strong-minded, and beautiful. The youngest, Josephine, died in Paris of tuberculosis while a maiden and only touched Cissy's life in that Cissy was christened Elinor Josephine. But Cissy lost the middle name anyway when her mother suspected Aunt Josephine of alienating her husband's affections. The middle Medill sister, Elinor, was Cissy's mother. The eldest, Katherine, a truly awesome woman, married Robert Sanderson McCormick, the nephew of Cyrus McCormick, her father's worst enemy.

The Medills were one of the several most important families in late-nineteenth-century Chicago. Aside from publishing the *Tribune* and influencing politics at Springfield, Mr. Medill had been Chicago's "fireproof" mayor.

Many Chicagoans disapproved of him and his fiery politics. Periodically he flung insults on his editorial page, reserving his choicest epithets for the most prominent citizens, such as Cyrus McCormick, who, he said had stolen the invention of the reaper from another man. Among those who disliked Joseph Medill was Cissy's paternal grandfather, Dr. Robert Wilson Patterson, who was particularly alarmed by Medill's "black Republican" vehemence on the slavery question.

Cissy's Grandfather Patterson was a Presbyterian minister whose parents had moved to Illinois from South Carolina because they could not live with slavery. Although an apostle of William Lloyd Garrison in his youth, Patterson became a moderate who worked hard to reconcile Northern and Southern factions within his church. In Chicago he became minister to the influential congregation of the Second Presbyterian Church. Then, after the fire, he led his flock to the village of Lake Forest, where he founded Lake Forest College. The community later became the city's most fashionable suburb.

Dr. Patterson was dismayed when his son and namesake, Robert Wilson Patterson, Jr., went to work as a reporter for Joseph Medill's *Tribune*. He had wanted his son to go into the church or, failing that, law. Young Patterson had enrolled in law school after graduation from Williams College, but the Chicago Fire had wiped out his father's capital and forced him to take a job. While he was working for the *Tribune*, "Rob" fell in love with the boss's daughter, Elinor, who was fresh from European grand tours, Miss Porter's School in Farmington, Connecticut, and debutante cotillions. Joseph Medill denied permission for them to marry, so did Dr. Patterson, and yet (doubtless at Elinor's instigation, for she was the headstrong one) they eloped.

Her marriage was a staggering disappointment to Elinor Patterson. She had been brought up on the crest of her father's success, and while her parents were stern disciplinarians, she and her sisters had been spoiled with material things and a sense of their own importance. They believed that nothing was too good for them. Rapidly Elinor and her sister Katherine decided that their husbands were not nearly good enough.

Rob Patterson succeeded better with his father-in-law than he did with his wife. Joseph Medill, recognizing Patterson's imagination and sound editorial judgement, designated him as his successor as editor of the *Tribune*. Patterson's job was a thankless one with little glory attached; he did the day-to-day work and Medill, who was largely absent, got the credit. When she spoke of her father years later, Cissy usually began with, "He was a hell of a good newspaperman."

The Patterson marriage was distinctly Victorian. Apparently they fell out of love as newlyweds, during the short time they lived on Mr. Patterson's salary and before Mr. Medill gave them a house and an allowance. Yet, of course, they never considered divorce. They referred to one another as Mr. Patterson and Mrs. Patterson, and they phrased their cruelties in formal language. Mrs. Patterson made independent decisions because, in financial terms, she could afford to. Mr. Patterson got quietly drunk in the stable and spent most of his leisure time at the all-male Chicago Club, playing cards and talking politics.

Two people scarcely could have been more incompatible than Cissy's parents, and their fortitude in enduring one another for close to forty years was remarkable. Rob Patterson was a restrained, reflective, melancholy gentleman. He was always trying to put things into perspective and order. Tall and slender, with a handsome, sensitive face, he hid a touch of the poet beneath his doggedly respectable attitudes and manners. He was a sweet man. "Nellie" Patterson, by contrast, caused commotion endemically. She was a large woman to start and she grew larger. Mrs. Patterson exploded with nervous energy and spoke loudly, though mercifully in a low register. She was voraciously ambitious for power, position, and material things, and there is no doubt she wished she had been born a man. As it was, in an era in which women were denied legitimate outlets for their ambitions, she succeeded nevertheless in expressing hers by storming the social citadels of the Atlantic Seaboard.

The single most consistent irritant in the Patterson marriage was Cissy's Aunt Kate McCormick, or "Kate the curst" as Mr. Patterson called her. Shrewder, brighter, more elegant, and even more ambitious than Mrs. Patterson, Kate took lifetime pleasure in upstaging her sister. "I *told you* not to marry Rob Patterson," she liked to say. In fact, Kate was dreadfully jealous of her brother-in-law's position at the *Tribune,* and she staged many plots designed to cost him his job. When Mr. Patterson died, Kate, whose husband still lived, pointed to her sister's widow's weeds at the funeral and hissed, "Nellie sure got ahead of me that time!"

Mrs. Patterson and Mrs. McCormick warred over hundreds of issues, including political favors and family jewels, but their most serious battle was fought over whose children would succeed to power at the *Chicago Tribune* after Joseph Medill died. The consuming rivalry between the sisters shaped the lives of their children.

Cissy, her older brother Joseph Medill Patterson, and her first cousins (Joseph) Medill and Robert Rutherford McCormick, came into a world dominated by two willful women. The father figure in their lives was their titanic old Grandfather Medill, who, coincidentally, was the source of the silver spoons in their mouths.

Chicago, the city which had brought their family to fortune, was still raw and hungry. The brick buildings were new, so was the lakefront, jacked up and filled in on the profits of land speculation, grain speculation, cattle speculation, railroad speculation, and other daring gambles which had made ruffians into tycoons. Here, between endless prairie to the west and an inland sea to the east, the city's fathers and mothers were building a little windbreaker of palaces, some French, some Venetian, some Gothic, some a bit of each. For art the city looked not to New York but to Paris. Chicago wanted to be the Paris of the New World. It lusted for elegance and opulence to soften the strident virility of its setting.

Cissy was born on November 7, 1881, when the United States was in the middle of the industrial revolution, and Chicago, just ten years after the Great Fire had destroyed it, had rebuilt itself and become the second most important commercial city in the country. The year of Cissy's birth saw the publication of Henry George's treatise *Progress and Poverty*, which inveighed against the unequal distribution of wealth and its effects on popular government, anticipating the Chicago Haymarket Riot of 1886 when a strike at the McCormick Reaper Works set off bombs and bullets. Meantime, Ulysses Grant was complaining about the diminution of the American frontier which, he said, dampened American initiative. Cissy was born at the moment of the fulfillment and the death of a dream—having found the pot of gold at the end of the rainbow, Americans were fashioning a golden calf.

But the social upheaval scarcely touched Cissy and her brother and her McCormick cousins, who were raised in a manner as artificial as an English manor house in the middle of a cornfield. Their mothers intended them to be "aristocrats." They lived in secluded nurseries under the supervision of governesses, and they suffered in elaborate clothes, starched and stiff as royalty at a garden party. The boys wore Little Lord Fauntleroy suits and shoulder-length curls until they went to school. Diction lessons blurred their Midwestern twangs, all except Joe Patterson's. Joe decided very early that nothing was going to make him elegant.

Cissy was a nervous, responsive baby with a delicate digestion. Her first portrait photograph shows a precociously stubborn expression and bright, wary eyes. At age three she was, in her own words, "already *fierce*." To her mother's disappointment Cissy was not beautiful, though she had inherited the Patrick red hair. Like her father she was small-boned and slender and brown-eyed. She stood up very straight. "You would, too, if your mother made you walk around with a book on your head," she later explained. Her natural grace and studied manners made her a star at her mother's teas, where guests called her "a little princess."

Her rebellion against her mother began very early. Awed by her mother's beauty and stunned by her insensitivity, Cissy became a problem child. She told lies and threw tantrums. Mrs. Patterson, never delicate in human relations, tried to bend Cissy into submission by old-fashioned disciplinary measures. Cissy learned how to make herself sick in order to get attention. Knowing this, when the child threw up all over a brand-new yellow coat from Paris, her mother simply slapped her in the face. Cissy grew to resent her mother's looks even more than her mother resented Cissy for not being pretty. Once, in a temper, she smashed her mother's favorite photograph.

The best way to annoy her mother, Cissy discovered, was to make up to her father. Robert Patterson thought it enchantingly feminine of his daughter to climb on his lap and swear that her papa was the most wonderful man in the whole world. When she pleaded for money and pets, she could make him believe, at least for a little while, that his was the world to give her if he chose. He could not help but laugh at the homely little tales she told behind her mother's back.

Cissy, her older brother Joe complained, was a chronic tattletale, always getting people into trouble. Joe, who was a sturdy, stubborn, straightforward little boy, yearned to escape the constant companionship of his baby sister and play with the neighborhood kids. With his father's help he beat down his mother's objections to his associating with "common children"—after all, a boy had to be sent to school when he became six. It was easier for her mother to "shelter" Cissy from the streets and the classrooms—a girl could be tutored at home.

The isolation of Cissy's early childhood was compounded by her mother's opinion that she would pick up vulgar habits if she hung around the kitchen with the servants. Cissy loved the kitchen, the amusing gossip she heard the Irish girls discussing on the back porch, the smell of strong coffee and clean wood. Despite her mother's dictates, she escaped to the kitchen whenever she saw her mother's carriage depart. The hired girls, who needed their jobs, told her to play somewhere else, and so, when Joe went to school, she spent much of her spare time reading books and drawing pictures.

Cissy preferred traveling to staying in Chicago. She liked to sun on Bailey's Beach at Newport and pick blueberries in Bar Harbor. Mrs. Patterson and Mrs. McCormick never enjoyed these resorts as much as their children did, because they worked so hard at staffing enormous rented houses, wangling memberships to clubs, enticing the snobs to attend their parties, and overcoming snubs.

Mrs. Patterson, restless as a ship in full sail, towed her children all over North America and Europe, but Cissy's favorite places were New Philadelphia, Ohio, where her Patrick cousins lived, and East Pasadena, California, where her Grandfather Medill, who suffered from arthritis and could no longer endure Chicago winters, had bought a big farm.

In California and at Mr. Medill's summer farm, Red Oaks, in Wheaton, Illinois, Cissy became knowledgeable about animals. She had loved them since her father had given her the first of a procession of puppies, and she had a way with them. "My hens, my pup, and my pony leave me hardly no time to go to bed," she bragged. Her grandfather, who had been quite a horseman in his day, schooled her in riding. "Grandfather is teaching me an awful lot," she wrote home from California, referring not only to animal studies but to her grandfather's lectures on world history and the freedom of the press.

When she became an adolescent, Cissy's charm deserted her. She was what was called "a late bloomer." She particularly despised her flat chest. Every time she looked at herself in the mirror, a gangly girl with a blotchy face and an unpleasant expression, she remembered that her mother, at the same age, had been "fully developed." Misery drove young Cissy to creative pursuits. In 1894, at thirteen, she sketched a girl sitting alone in fog—a strong portrait that conveyed her sense of isolation. She wrote melancholy poems, inspired by a copious reading of romantic novels. Her Aunt Kate McCormick, just to be devilish, allowed Cissy to borrow "risqué" books like *Vanity Fair* and *Boule de Suif,* knowing that Cissy's mother periodically searched her children's rooms for offending literature. Inevitably Mrs. Patterson would find the books and demand to know the meaning of her sister's behavior. And Mrs. McCormick would answer in her withering baritone, "There's nothing in any of those books that Cissy doesn't already know and probably practice," an effective if untruthful retort.

Cissy was fifteen before her mother took her schooling seriously. Education, Cissy's parents agreed, was a masculine matter. (They took Cissy's brother's education so seriously that they sent him to Groton at the age of eleven, where he was brutally hazed for his midshipman's suit with brass buttons, his Midwest accent, and his general arrogance.) In the autumn of 1896 Cissy went away to Miss Hersey's School on Beacon Street in Boston—the city Mrs. Patterson considered the most socially desirable. It was expected that Cissy would acquire a New England patina. Her grandfather warned her, "I look for a rapid polish on your manners, because, like rosewood and sugar maple, you have a grain susceptible of taking an elegant one."

The intellectual climate of the school was dry and Cissy's brief thirst for knowledge disappeared there. She found the work easy. She read rapidly enough to absorb most lessons within a few minutes, and so she was left free to daydream about beaux and clothes and parties. Having her older brother Joe and her cousin Medill McCormick at Yale gave her immediate status with the other girls. Despite the dour reports she sent home about the brutal headmistress, the inedible food, and the crushing work load, she managed to construct a pleasant life for herself at Miss Hersey's. Pelting her father with breathless requests for money, she accumulated enough cash to bribe the school's houseman and chambermaid to do her daily chores and still had enough left over to pay for theater tickets and other extras. On holidays she always had an invitation to visit a girlfriend in Manchester or Washington.

The year that Cissy graduated from Miss Hersey's she and her brother and cousins posed for a picture with their Grandfather Medill, who was by now deaf and arthritic. The photograph marks the end of an era in the family, because the following year, the year that the United States entered the Spanish-American War, Mr. Medill died and a tribal interregnum ensued. The old man looked as keen as an eagle at his last sitting, and the eyes of his four grandchildren mirrored the defiance of his gaze. The young Medills—Medill McCormick, twenty-one, Joseph Medill Patterson, nineteen, Elinor Medill Patterson, seventeen, and Robert Rutherford McCormick, eighteen—were a remarkable group of adolescents, who clearly belonged together. Their smooth, plump, healthy faces carried the same disturbing expression of arrogance, belligerence, and intelligence. Except for their clothes, snowy linen collars, and starched cuffs, they might have been a team of resistance fighters. From the photograph they seem to be saying, "we are rich, young, beautiful, and Medill."

The three boys and the old man were all slightly in love with Cissy. Mr. Medill had designated her as the only direct heir among his grandchildren. Under the terms of his will she was to receive ten shares of *Tribune* stock outright, while the boys were left to beg from their mothers. He disapproved of spoiled, arrogant boys and expressed extreme displeasure when Joe Patterson, the reckless one, ran off to Shanghai during the spring term of his junior year at Yale to report on the Boxer Rebellion— for William Randolph Hearst of all people!

Joe considered himself to be a much more respectable character than his sister Cissy, whom he criticized as being frivolous, but he had a healthy respect for her just the same. He admired her "guts," and she knew how to make him laugh. Medill McCormick, a more dignified and genteel young man, entertained a chaste and romantic feeling for his cousin Cissy. He called her *la princesse lointaine*, and he discouraged her suitors. Medill's little brother, "Bert," was younger than Cissy and she made him stammer. Although he found her glamorous, Bert did not like her very well—she teased him mercilessly and called him "Bert the Swipe."

In 1899, when her Grandfather Medill died, Cissy was at Miss Porter's School in Farmington, Connecticut, being "finished," and it was her cousin "Bert" who was at Mr. Medill's deathbed at the ranch in San Antonio. It was he who reported that Mr. Medill's last words had been "What's the news?"—about the Spanish American War. Since his family had not yet learned to appreciate young Bert, they never thanked him for creating the family's favorite legend.* Bert did not even enter into the frantic calculations which Joseph Medill's death occasioned. As the less-attractive younger brother of Medill McCormick, his name was passed over in the nominations for future publisher of the *Tribune*. Of course no one considered Cissy either, since she was a girl. The race was between Medill McCormick and Cissy's brother Joe, though in the meantime Cissy's father continued to run the newspaper, as he had been doing since Old Man Medill's retirement in 1893.

Cissy came back from Farmington for her grandfather's funeral in Chicago. All the public schools and city offices closed for the day. The flags flew at half staff. Joseph Medill was buried next to his wife in the large plot he had bought at Graceland Cemetery. During the burial ceremony Mrs. McCormick said with satisfaction, "That's where we'll all be someday." But in the meantime Katherine McCormick meant to make the most of her remaining time. And she began at once.

Joseph Medill had accumulated 51 per cent of Chicago

---

* Robert Rutherford McCormick's acute sense of family history became a mania, when, as publisher of the *Tribune,* he treated readers and radio audiences to precise accounts of each major family event, including, for example, his own birth.

Tribune Company stock and he left his holdings in trust to his two living daughters, Mrs. McCormick and Mrs. Patterson. Knowing their temperaments, Medill tried to write a will which would afford the girls a handsome income but protect the *Tribune* from their interference. Legal fine points, however, inconvenienced Katherine McCormick, so she ignored them. Although she had moved into the Joseph Medill mansion in Chicago, she was bored with the city and tired of grand tours. She wanted a real position. Without any shame, she represented herself to President William McKinley, whom she knew slightly through Mark Hanna, as the *Chicago Tribune*'s principal stockholder and spokesman. The President owed a political debt to the *Tribune* and he repaid it by appointing Katherine McCormick's husband minister to the Austro-Hungarian court. Robert Patterson, as editor-in-chief of the newspaper, found himself in the unfortunate position of accepting a political bribe on behalf of his despised sister-in-law. The Patterson family was perfectly furious.

Cissy's mother, never the schemer her sister Kate was, could think of no more imaginative way to capitalize on her inheritance than to build another mansion, this time in Washington. She already owned the imposing square brown palazzo with a studded door which defended the northwest corner of Astor Street and Burton Place on Chicago's Near North Side; Joseph Medill had commissioned architect Stanford White to build it for her at the same time that he gave Kate his own house. But no mansion could keep a Medill sister home, Mrs. Patterson moved operations to Washington for the same reason that Mrs. Marshall Field and Mrs. Levi Leiter and Mrs. Ed-

ward Walsh were erecting pleasure palaces there. Unlike
Boston or New York or Charleston, Washington was the
one city in the East where any woman with money and
talent could set up housekeeping and become an important hostess.

Cissy was eighteen and in her second year at Miss
Porter's School when her mother paid $83,000 for a piece
of swampy land on Washington's still undeveloped Dupont Circle and spent another $200,000 on the house.
Cissy and her father heartily agreed that the project was
ridiculous. Kate McCormick predicted that if her sister
should try living on Dupont Circle, she would undoubtedly die from malaria. But Mrs. Patterson pointed out
that a number of other fashionable people, including the
incredibly rich Mrs. Leiter (the family was in grain),
were also building on the Circle.

The house that Stanford White designed for her turned
out to be an opulent but tasteful expression of his client's
personality. It had a beautiful façade of white stone and
variegated marble ornamentation with a curved frontage
embracing the park. It was pretentious; its street number,
Fifteen, appeared in stonework above the entrance like a
royal coat of arms. The old French fireplaces, the Louis
XVI ballroom, the fruitwood paneling in the drawing
room, the pegged rosewood floor in the dining room, the
doorknobs of semiprecious stones, the grillwork on the
ascenseur, were direct financial statements.

Her mother's new palace depressed Cissy. She was at a
sensitive age and felt keenly that her mother should be
taking care of her father, who was in poor health. Cissy
knew that her father was quietly drinking himself into
serious trouble and that his depressions had grown more

severe. He looked bad and went into coughing fits. It made her desperately sad to see him go off on rest cures all by himself, and though she hated herself for it, she could not bring herself to accompany him to the train stations on these occasions. She said she could not bear to stand around on platforms feeling "extremely large-sized and in the way."

Cissy herself became ill while at Farmington and had to be taken out of school. Her disease confounded precise diagnosis. She suffered from extreme nervous tension which brought on fainting spells, dizziness, and odd palpitations of the heart. The doctors recommended a change of climate, and so, accompanied by a trained nurse, a *mademoiselle,* and a cook, she was sent south to Thomasville, Georgia, the hunting resort.

Cissy spent an entire season in Thomasville, though she recovered her health in less than a month. She enjoyed the situation. At nineteen she was mistress of her own house and her own time. She studied a certain number of hours with her French *mademoiselle,* who also chaperoned her, but that seemed a small price to pay for the days she spent on the hunting field. She excelled at fox hunting, and she and her horse Exclusive won a collection of foxtail brushes, the reward for being first at the kill. Cissy rode so lightly in her sidesaddle that she made the awesome business of taking high fences in that position look natural and easy.

Though strictly a society resort, Thomasville maintained a deliberate atmosphere of rusticity, and Cissy led a leisurely, athletic, happy existence there. She met plenty of young men. Her brother came down from Yale for holidays, bringing roommates and friends. But Joe and cousin Medill McCormick remained Cissy's favorite men; she could not decide which was handsomer.

In the winter of 1901, however, Mrs. Patterson decided that Cissy must come home to Chicago for her formal presentation to society. At her New Year's coming-out tea at the Astor Street mansion, she appeared in a fragile pink chiffon dress with her copper hair piled high on her head. As a debutante Cissy was a ravishing creature, still not beautiful because of her odd features, but slim and light and with delicate coloring. Her presence exerted such a powerful effect on boys that she grew to accept extravagant compliments casually. "Oh," she would say, "you must love me for my Grecian nose"; she referred to herself as "the bird of paradise."

Now that Cissy had become remarkably attractive and a great belle, her mother underwent what Cissy called "the old metamorphosis" and developed a sudden but passionate interest in her daughter. With her own beauty faded and her once proud figure turned to fat, Mrs. Patterson took charge of Cissy's social career with all the dedication of a stage mother. She charged into Cissy's room in the mornings and flooded her with conversation during breakfasts, until Cissy became unpleasant about it. The child offered scarcely a thank you for the gowns from Worth of Paris and the pearls from Cartier. It was unbearable, Cissy felt, that the full force of Mrs. Patterson's personality should be turned on her young life. Besides, it was too late. Long years of insensitive neglect had hardened Cissy permanently against her mother, and nothing Mrs. Patterson could do or say would erase them.

With what she considered Cissy's well-being in mind

(a good marriage), Mrs. Patterson endeavored to protect Cissy from the follies of youth. She opened and read the mail addressed to Miss Patterson. She periodically rifled Cissy's belongings, including her private papers. She forced Cissy's chaperones to give detailed reports of her behavior—who danced with her, who flirted, what was said about her, and so forth.

Cissy's favorite beau was Frederick McLaughlin, a handsome blond boy who was on the Yale polo team with Joe Patterson. All the girls of Cissy's year admired Freddy, but Freddy loved Cissy. Cissy's mother disapproved of the romance; she said that Freddy's father used to deliver groceries at the back door before making his coffee fortune. Freddy and Cissy liked to go riding together along Lake Michigan, and to discourage Freddy's suit Mrs. Patterson hid Cissy's riding clothes.

Cissy observed that she could always stay one step ahead of her mother, who was persistent but not exactly subtle. She had been telling lies to her ever since she could remember, and now she lied frighteningly well. Mrs. Patterson might wait up in her dressing gown, hair streaming down her back like Lady Macbeth, until Cissy came home from debutante parties, but after Mrs. Patterson finally went to bed Cissy sneaked out and went riding along the lake. And where deception failed, a direct assault sometimes succeeded. Cissy discovered that her mother, for all her bluff and bluster, was vulnerable to ridicule. Cissy could imitate her voice and caricature her manner so cruelly that the unfortunate woman would break into uncharacteristic tears.

For several reasons Mrs. Patterson accepted her sister Kate's invitation for Cissy to visit the McCormicks in

Vienna and be presented at the Austro-Hungarian court. The Pattersons thought it "a scandal" that Robert S. Mc-Cormick was the American minister there, and Mrs. Patterson had been making sarcastic remarks all over Washington and Chicago about the palace which her sister Kate had rented for herself. On the other hand she realized that it was a great opportunity for Cissy to be presented at the most exclusive court in Europe. Except for the children of diplomats the only young ladies who were invited to court were those whose titles stretched back seven generations. Mrs. Patterson rather fancied the idea of Cissy marrying a title. And it seemed "only fair" that the Pattersons should get *some* advantage out of McCormick's appointment, since he owed it to the *Tribune.*

"Vienna," Cissy wrote home in the spring of 1902, "is the prettiest, gayest, most frivolous place one could imagine." There were race meets and balls and opera parties, teas and grouse shoots and picnics in the Vienna Woods. After a little coaching from her Aunt Kate she mastered the rigid Spanish etiquette of the court, and she said that being American gave her an advantage over "the little countesses," who struck her as a "herd of simple sheep." Cissy managed to flirt enough while keeping her eyes down, and she attracted a following among the young officers in their shining boots and gold epaulettes, but *"Tiens!"* she cried, "These men are so constrained in female company!"

Then, at a dinner dance, across a room filled with people, she saw an older man who was not in uniform—a tall, thin, arrogant Pole. His eyes were black and predatory under thick black eyebrows. He affected long curly hair and a long curly mustache. He was amusing a crowd of ladies and everything about him, from the cut of his clothes to the sweep of his gestures, was exaggerated, as if he were on stage. Count Josef Gizycki was his name. Cissy caught his eye and felt faint. For such a playboy, and Cissy identified him immediately as a member of that close little set, the man was astonishingly primitive. Without waiting for an introduction, he walked across the room and presented himself to Cissy and she fell in love. As she wrote later, "she felt her fingertips turn icy cold" and "her heart began to beat in heavy, sickening thuds."

Cissy's Aunt Kate McCormick, of course, immediately grilled her niece about what had gone on. Mrs. McCormick, a great believer in research, unearthed the information that Count Josef Gizycki was a man old enough to be Cissy's father and "one of the most dangerous men in the empire." The Gizycki title dated from the ninth century in Poland and his mother had served as lady-in-waiting to the Empress' mother, but the Count was not considered a fit companion for a nice girl. He was at least 35 and probably closer to 45. His exploits as an officer in the Austrian cavalry were well known. Aside from making a name for himself by participating in the famous horseback chase from Berlin to Vienna, the Count had spent his army career gambling and seducing women. It was said that he had fathered children from Russia to England. Since retiring from the army, Gizycki had been lounging around the spas and capitals of Europe, drinking and gambling, while his landed estates, scattered around partitioned Poland under several dominions, went to wreck and ruin. "If we should meet him again, I'll drop a hint that you haven't got a cent," said Mrs. McCormick to Cissy.

Although President Theodore Roosevelt transferred Ambassador McCormick from Vienna to St. Petersburg, just when Mrs. McCormick had redecorated the embassy, Cissy continued to meet Count Josef Gizycki. Because of his confused political allegiances the Count was attached to Czar Nicholas' court as well as Franz Josef's. The McCormicks alerted Mrs. Patterson to the danger of Gizycki's interest, but Mrs. Patterson could not help being rather pleased. Gizycki's lineage impressed her very much. Cissy's father said he would sooner see the girl in Hell before he would see her make such a match, but his influence in the family had waned.

In 1903, when Cissy was back in America and spending the summer with her mother in Lake Forest, Illinois, Count Gizycki wrote to the Pattersons asking for Cissy's hand in marriage. Mrs. Patterson did not know what to make of the situation. She could not decide whether her sister Kate had invented a salacious reputation for the Count just to be malicious. After all, she mused, it would be comforting to see Cissy settled down, especially in some nice castle surrounded by people of quality and by all those nice horses she loved so dearly, and Gizycki owned race horses. On the other hand, Poland was so far away. Would the man expect a dowry? Mrs. Patterson finally decided it would not do any harm "to show these foreigners that some American girls were not available for the mere asking." She replied with a brisk note indicating that his attentions were premature. She hinted with her customary tactlessness that she was disappointed by his financial situation. "Is it true," she inquired, "that you have dissipated several fortunes?"

"My little Filly," Gizycki wrote to Cissy in his illegible, childish scrawl. "Go and tell Mamma that you have made up your mind to marry and I will kiss your gold hair."

Cissy persuaded her mother that she must be allowed at least to go back to Europe. Mrs. Patterson wanted to meet the "young man" and so she relented, though to insure Cissy's protection she brought along one of her inexhaustible supply of impoverished cousins, whose duty it became to dog Cissy's footsteps. Cousin Mary's reward was free passage and second-class rooms at first-class hotels.

When she met Josef Gizycki in Paris, Mrs. Patterson had to admit that he was charming. She nearly consented then and there. But she changed her mind and shipped Cissy off with Mary to Baden-Baden. Cissy spent three months moving from resort to resort, with Gizycki in hot, if erratic pursuit. Chasing after "little girls" grew boring, he admitted, once the novelty had worn off.

Mrs. Patterson still had not consented when she took Cissy back to America for Christmas, 1903. She wanted Cissy to take advantage of the Dupont Circle house which, after a fire and other mishaps, was at last ready for occupancy. Although at twenty-two Cissy was slightly past debutante age, her mother thought it would be nice for her to come out in Washington.

"Watch the way that girl moves," said Theodore Roosevelt to his daughter Alice Lee Roosevelt as Cissy came down a receiving line at the White House. "She moves as *no one* has ever moved before!" Cissy made an impact on Washington Society that winter. Her mother gave her several lavish parties, with French champagne and the Marine Band, and Miss Roosevelt accepted her in the "Cabinet Circle," an informally arranged but strictly secluded group which included a very few young ladies and all the eligible men in Washington. Cissy became friends with the President's lively daughter and with another reigning belle, Countess Marguerite Cassini, the fascinating daughter of the Russian Ambassador. Together they were known as the Three Graces of Washington. Later Evalyn Walsh McLean replaced the Countess as the Second Grace.

It was charming to be a princess in Washington, but Cissy still insisted that she must marry Gizycki. And so, in February of 1904, Mrs. Patterson wired him in care of the Vienna Jockey Club and gave her consent. "I must confess I am relieved," the Count wrote to Cissy. "It is all very well to play smart but sensitive flirt in cold blood, but this time, all the time since I left you, I wasn't a moment happy or content, though I arranged and managed my little affairs perfectly."

Among those who disapproved of the match were Cissy's father, her brother, and an old love, Clive Runnels, who wrote her: "It is probably better than having you elope, although that would be a stronger finish. . . . Dear, Cissy, be a bit thoughtful of your husband. . . . You would be much happier if you would do more to make others happy. One more thing—give up flirting! You are old enough to stop!"

Her friends generally agreed that she was making a mistake, but Cissy's only close girl friend was her cousin Medill's bride, Ruth Hanna McCormick. Cissy had known Ruth from childhood, when she and her family had visited Mark Hanna, the Republican "kingmaker," in Thomasville. Ruth and Cissy had been at Miss Porter's together, and except for the fact that Cissy would have been jealous of any girl married to her beloved cousin, she trusted Ruth. Ruth tried all through the night before the wedding to convince Cissy to change her mind before it was too late, but Cissy would not listen. She bragged that she knew all about Gizycki's mistresses and that she did not care. "Suppose he *is* marrying me for my money and my virginity?" she demanded. "I love him."

Cissy's family, as they gathered in Washington for the wedding, remarked to one another that Cissy took a non-chalant attitude toward the estate she was about to enter. They were embarrassed when Cissy arrived late to her wedding rehearsal because she had been out horseback riding with an ardent beau named Bonaparte, a descendant of Napoleon. Mrs. Patterson announced that she was a nervous wreck and told Cissy several times that when and if the marriage failed, she must come right home. "Darling," she said, "remember that you can always come back to Chicago." Cissy had no intention of coming back to Chicago. She hated home now that her father was melancholy and her brother was married to pretty little Alice Higinbotham and Medill was married to Ruth.

At noon on Thursday, April 14, 1904, in a Roman Catholic ceremony in the drawing room of Fifteen Dupont Circle, witnessed by thirty-five people, including Pattersons, McCormicks, the President's daughter, and representatives of several embassies, Eleanor Medill Patterson became the Countess Gizycka. During the wedding breakfast a rumor circulated through the company that Gizycki had deserted Cissy because the Pattersons had refused

Cissy a dowry. However, after a distressing interval, the best man, Ivan Rubido-Zichy, announced that Gizycki had gone to his hotel to change his clothes and was at the train station waiting for Cissy. Head held high, Cissy drove off with her father in the bridal carriage, which the guests had decorated with bells and orange blossoms.

2

Castles in Poland

The romantic half of Cissy became disillusioned on her honeymoon with Josef Gizycki. She was thin and pale at the end of a two-month wedding trip, or *"Flitterwochen"* as Gizy called it, through the spas and capitals of Europe. She looked ill enough to cause speculation that she was already pregnant, a rumor which to her own relief and her husband's disappointment had no basis.

During their courtship she had dismissed all the warnings against marrying a man from such a different background. Now she was not so sure. She found herself longing for a Sunday bicycle ride to the Saddle and Cycle Club with Freddy McLaughlin, to sit with him on the edge of the dock and dangle her bare feet into Lake Michigan, and eat an ice cream cone. Freddy always made her feel relaxed. With Gizy she felt as stiff as a corset. Gizy was like a code she could not quite decipher. From her copious reading of romantic novels she knew how true lovers communicated by affectionate little gestures and meaningful glances. Yet she and Gizy could not seem to exchange the simplest thoughts without misunderstanding one another. He spoke English rapidly and charmingly, like a three year old. She spoke German like an American schoolgirl. As for Russian, now the official language of eastern Poland, she was still struggling with the alphabet. Like diplomats, they met each other halfway, in French or English, and, as in diplomacy, the compromise was not ideal.

Cissy and Gizy spent their wedding night in a monumental suite at the New York Ritz, which set a forbidding mood that was further darkened when Gizy strolled off to his suite for a cigar. When he did visit her room, he took her, or so she remembered, "without one word or caress," then left her to cry alone.

If unnerving in love, Gizy was certainly an alarming companion. He could be extremely amusing, she acknowledged that. He flourished in public. When they went with his friends, whether driving through the Präter or boating on the Seine, he kept everyone entertained with his capers and wicked little asides. Cissy enjoyed going to restaurants with him; headwaiters greeted him with the deference due a free-spending aristocrat. In public, he wore Cissy on his arm like a jewel, and she adored him.

But Cissy was too young to cope with a Gizy. She could not anticipate his moods. One moment he would be smiling compliments, the next moment, for no apparent reason, his face would darken and he would turn on her saying, "Don't bore me, please don't bore me." Cissy could not keep him amused; he was liable to get up from the dinner table during the soup course if he was annoyed with the company, the service, or the menu.

Gizy believed in the most fashionable antidotes to relieve boredom: drinking and gambling. When the fever was with him, he sent Cissy to her room and she did not see him again until he got out of bed the next afternoon. Several mornings she heard him fumbling with his door key, so she knew he came home very late, and she also understood the teasing references of his friends to wild nights in the casinos. She remembered that five weeks after their wedding, when they were staying at the Sacher Hotel in Vienna, he banged on her door at five A.M. and demanded $11,000. She finally gave it to him when he threatened to go to the usurers.

Previously only her mother had been able to frighten Cissy like that. Though quite unafraid of most physical dangers, Cissy was sensitive to spoken insults. She had a horror of being made to feel "awkward and in the way." Gizy could always make her feel gauche. One morning she thought to surprise him by going to his room for breakfast. Dressed in her best peignoir, she sailed through his door without knocking and discovered him with his curls set under a black skullcap and his mustache tied to his ears with rubber and wire. She stared open-mouthed at this apparition with the blazing eyes. Then, not knowing whether to laugh or cry, she backed out and slammed the door behind her. Neither of them mentioned the incident again.

There were already more unmentionable than mentionable topics in their marriage. One reliable subject was horses, another was fashionable gossip, a third was gossip about fashion, and often all three came together. Gizy's keenest ambition was to build up a really fine racing stable and a first-class hunt, with top English hounds and clubhouses for his guests. It would be expensive, he explained, but he considered the expense justified. Anticipating the future, he took time out in London to expand his collection of riding clothes to include another pair of custom-made Peel boots and a pink coat cut so tight that only the tailor's genius stopped it from wrinkling.

Cissy was not afraid of competing with Gizy's women friends, who wore diamonds as if they were daisies. Cissy, after all, had the advantage of youth and freshness. It was Gizy who bothered her. He changed his clothes several times a day and was so vain about his hands that he continually kept them gloved. He avoided touching so much as the arms of a chair when he sat down. Narcissus himself might have admired the way Gizy could pick out his reflection in any available surface, including shop-windows, rain puddles, and other people's eyeglasses. Cissy could not compete. She suspected he washed his hands after touching her, and the suspicion infuriated her.

Despite a certain disillusionment about her lover, Cissy was in a good mood on the June morning that she accompanied him for the first time on a bouncing *britchka* from the railroad depot at Proskurow, a Ukranian garrison town halfway between Warsaw and Odessa, to one of his estates near Starconstantin in Novasilicia. She chattered happily for most of the six-hour drive. The Orient was visible on the horizon. Spring came late to southern Russia. The meadowlarks were in flight and the fields, touched by green, were creamed spinach to the milky sky, while old peasant women trudging under their bundles looked like a lovely procession of nuns. Cissy spotted a blue church dome and asked Gizy whether he didn't think it looked like an onion, and when she saw the crude wooden crosses which the peasants erected everywhere, she thought of scarecrows back in Illinois. The sun shone warmly; and Gizy's coachman sported a crown of peacock feathers in his hat in honor of the occasion.

Later, when she described that day, Cissy omitted the sunshine and substituted other things that had seemed unimportant at the time—swarming black flies, the old Jew at the station who whined at Gizy about unpaid loans, the diseased dogs and children peering out of the mud clusters which Gizy called his villages. When a peasant girl hurled herself at Cissy's feet, she shrank back in revulsion, thinking the wretch might bite her, and not knowing the girl wanted to kiss the hem of her dress. In retrospect the whole day was an intentional mockery.

"It's not finished of course," Gizy remarked as they drove down an endless line of skinny poplars toward his castle. It was hard to see very clearly in the fading light, but Cissy could just make out a structure looming from an empty plain like a ghost from the sea. Even on this soft summer evening it cast a chill. It was not a castle, it was not even a house; it was a warehouse, and a deserted one at that.

Inside huge pieces of furniture tilted at alarming angles under the savage gaze of Gizy's ancestral portraits. A fire had dispelled neither the damp stale smell nor the chill. When she sat down on a cracked leather chair, Cissy noticed a little silk pillow which seemed, in this place, like a flower on a corpse. At that point she said she would like to go and rest before dinner.

When she entered the succession of badly proportioned and ill-appointed little alcoves which constituted her apartment, Cissy sniffed another woman's lingering presence. Someone had attempted cozy furniture arrangements; someone had scattered more of those little silk pillows; someone had left a strand of black hair in the washstand and a packet of hairpins in the bureau drawer. And no one, as Cissy's maid complained, no one had thought to clean up afterwards.

Cissy told Gizy that if he expected her to spend so much as one night in that woman's room, he had better think again, because she did not intend to put so much as a foot inside it. Gizy kept his composure. As she later described the scene, he raised his eyebrows and put on a tolerant, amused expression. But of course, he said, she was free to pick any room she liked; there was no shortage of rooms in the house. In fact, if it would make her happy, he would engage carpenters and masons to arrange new quarters for her in the wing that formerly belonged to his mother. Meantime she should calm herself with a glass of vodka and concentrate on pleasant subjects. He reminded her of the new horse he had bought for her and of the parties she would attend. As he had tried to tell her in so many different ways, he had been loved the whole of his life and the sooner she got used to it, the better.

The summer season, which opened like a rose-colored parasol, temporarily shaded the Gizyckis from their difficulties. These brief warm months, when the lilacs bloomed and willows fringed the ponds, were the occasion for the annual aristocratic migration from the capitals to the countryside. It was a time to sip tea on the green grass, to look over the accounts, a time to dance and to discipline the peasants. Cissy and Gizy were rarely alone.

Everyone agreed that life in the provinces was amusing in the right company but quite unbearable with no company. The manor houses were as isolated as oases in the desert. One could drive for hours through fields and forests without encountering anybody but peasants. To escape the disturbing solitude the nobility spent their weeks visiting and being visited, which made excellent sense since it kept one's servants busy and also eliminated the necessity of stopping at hotels when traveling back and forth between various estates. Gizy could go five hundred miles between his Ukranian lands and his Galician lands without ever having to worry about accommodations.

Like the American South in the eighteenth century, the partitioned Poland of 1905 was an aggregate of large rural holdings owned by a small number of aristocrats and worked by a large number of peasants. There was a small middle class, and the majority of shopkeepers, moneylenders, artisans, and merchants belonged to the despised Jewish race. More than 90 per cent of the population lived in the country since there was insufficient industry to attract workers to the cities. Though serfdom had been abolished for half a century, the unequal distribution of land and the well-entrenched feudal system kept the peasants in place.

A landowner like Gizy could punish one of his peasants in any way, whenever he wished. Once Cissy witnessed him thrash his coachman with a whip as punishment for steering the carriage into a rut. She was shocked at this brutality and by the discovery that Polish arisocrats used their peasant girls as casually as American plantation owners had once used their Negro women. It was reasonably easy to spot an aristocrat's bastard among the peasants. There was one little peasant boy on the Ukranian estate who Cissy swore was the spitting image of Gizy, tall and slim with an ivory complexion, but she could not be sure because Gizy seemed never to notice the child.

If this eighteenth-century existence seemed in some ways primitive to Cissy, she found it in other ways deliciously civilized. There was a voluptuous, indolent rhythm to the days and nights that made American life seem nervous and vulgar by contrast. One had all the time in the world to read and ride and eat and hold long conversations without feeling pressured to do something useful. One did not feel guilty about self-indulgence.

Even at an enormous houseparty the daily routine was as soothing as a slow waltz. At a great house like Lancut Castle which belonged to the practically royal Potockis, as many as fifty guests lived comfortably together for weeks at a time without getting restless. Count Josef Potocki and his intriguing wife Helene (Betka) collected the *haut de panier* of European aristocracy within their white stone walls and provided them with an endless procession of entertainments—concerts by the fifty-man stableboy band, masked balls, croquet, tennis, polo matches, and exotic meals in a series of eleven dining rooms. Breakfast was served in bed, luncheon was at two with coffee on the terrace afterward, tea was at five in the great hall, dinner at nine was followed by gambling in the gaming rooms and dancing in the ballroom. Guests did exactly as they pleased, and had only to wear the right clothes at the right time of day. Flirting was considered good form, and so were discreetly conducted love affairs. The host and hostess enjoyed their guests and behaved as if it was perfectly natural to entertain fifty people around the clock. An army of footmen in green livery and bare-foot women in native costumes performed their chores in a well-rehearsed drill.

When someone asked Countess Potocka how she housed so many servants, the Countess replied that she had never been down in her cellar to see the servants' quarters because she feared the smell and the germs. For the same delicate reason the Potocki family and its entourage occupied a balcony in the village church separated by glass from the rest of the congregation.

But the high style of life was costly and it made Cissy nervous that they were spending so much. Her Scotch-Irish ancestry rose up and protested against improvidence, yet what could she do? Gizy kept suggesting she solicit her father, but that was because he did not know her father very well. Meantime Gizy grumbled about his mortgages as if they were Cissy's fault, and he used them as an excuse to leave her alone for days at a time, explaining that unless the yield from his lands improved he would be forced to sell property which had belonged to his family for centuries. She tried, but she could not get interested in horse trading, wood cutting, fertilizer, and the rest of it.

As summer waned and the prevailing winds blew in from Russia, Cissy was ready to go to Vienna, or even Warsaw, where she could see people on the streets and go to restaurants and the theater. She felt that Gizy was punishing her by staying in the country. Why of all years had he picked this one to worry about his estates?

Nearing her twenty-fourth birthday, Cissy encountered solitude for the first time, and she hated it. When Gizy left her behind in Novasilicia, she had no one to talk to except her personal maid and the English stablemaster, because the peasants spoke only Polish, and, now that the Czar had ordered it, Russian. Cissy had no domestic chores, only the obligation to exercise her horses. The pleasure of riding grayed along with the autumn skies. Who wanted to ride alone day after day? When she heard herself asking the stablemaster to tea, she knew she was getting desperate. It hardly helped to read the novels she found mildewing in Gizy's library—they were all so gloomy.

Cissy identified with practically every literary heroine but especially with Dumas' tender prostitute in *La Dame aux Camélias* and with Tolstoy's spirited Countess Natasha in *War and Peace*. All summer she had been Natasha—so much more alive than everybody else. Now she was Camille—so much nearer to death than anyone suspected. She could not look at food without gagging, she was tired, and she felt so ill in the mornings that she stayed in bed till noon.

When, upon consulting a doctor in Vienna, Cissy discovered that she was pregnant, she really got sick. She did not want a baby, at least not now, and perhaps not ever. Nevertheless, in Blansko Castle in the Austro-Hungarian province of Moravia, on September 3, 1905, Cissy gave birth to a girl. Everyone had hoped for a boy. However, as Cissy's mother, who had attended the birth, wrote to her anxious father in Chicago, it was a perfect miracle that mother and child were alive after all the shocks of the preceding nine months.

Cissy's pregnancy had been eagerly greeted by Gizy, who had expected that the birth of a child would loosen the purse strings on the Patterson fortune. The pregnancy actually proved to be the end of their marriage. Cissy was weak most of the period, twice collapsing and once requiring a frantic sleigh ride from Gizycki's Ukrainian estate to a Vienna hospital. Gizy was disconcerted by his wife's physical ordeal and sought to banish the unpleasantness from his mind by absenting himself from her. Other troubles weighed in upon the Count. His estates were in a state of neglect, and unrest was sweeping through the peasant class of Russia and Eastern Europe. His answer to such problems was to spend more time drinking and gambling at the Vienna Jockey Club.

Cissy, left alone with a disgruntled Polish midwife and an impoverished American cousin sent over by Mrs. Patterson, brooded over her husband's wandering ways. Goaded by her suspicions, she broke into the Count's locked desk to look for a diary she knew he had been keeping since their wedding. Her worst fears were confirmed by the detailed listing of Gizy's romantic encounters—names, places, and dates. Gizycki protested truculently that his wife's spying was a sin worse than philandering, and their quarrels grew violent. Cissy considered her marriage "shattered" but decided she would be more miserable separated from her husband than if she accepted the humiliation. After the diary incident, however, Cissy didn't try to be a good wife. She renounced all domestic duties, including ordering meals and visiting her child's nursery, on the excuse that she was "*schlapp*," though she roused herself for parties and stag hunts. Aghast that any woman would dare to behave that way, Gizy berated her and beat her, but her behavior only worsened. She taunted him about his gambling and his women, and she laughed that he objected to her flirtations. One night in January of 1908, when they were staying at the hunting resort of Pau in the south of France, Cissy made a scene in front of Gizy's friends, sarcastically criticizing the techniques he was using to seduce his dinner partner. Afterward at their villa Gizy expressed his rage by battering his wife to her knees.

There was no riposte to such treatment but to retire from the field of battle, so, without giving notice, Cissy packed up two-year-old Felicia and the Polish nurse and fled to London, where she checked into the Savoy and boarded the baby and nanny in the suburb of Hampton Hills. Cissy led a frenzied life, running up enormous bills, entertaining and being entertained, rarely seeing her daughter, often finding her name linked with prominent English gentlemen. She alternated between spreading malicious gossip about Gizy and half-heartedly attempting a reconciliation.

In London, Cissy received a letter from Gizy saying, "It is impossible for me to live with you any longer. I do not want Felicia to have the sort of education of which you are the victim. Last-Love, Last-Time, Gizy."

Meantime, unknown to Cissy, Gizy was having her followed by private detectives whom he had hired to report on her activities and to find out where she was keeping Felicia. The detectives had to follow her for two weeks before she finally visited the baby in Hampton Hills. When Gizy heard that Countess Gizycka was gadding about London, neglecting their child, he filed in Vienna for an annulment on the grounds of desertion. Next, Cissy received a call from Hampton Hills and learned that three of Count Gizycki's detectives had kidnapped Felicia. When Cissy was able to contact Gizycki, he assured her that the child was safe but refused to tell any more than that. He did agree to have the baby brought to a house on the outskirts of Vienna where Cissy could visit her for an hour if she would come to Austria.

On the afternoon of April 27, 1908, Cissy arrived alone at the arranged meeting place, while six of her own detectives stationed themselves in surrounding shrubbery. Gizy's detectives were expecting a counterattack, however, and did not fall into the trap. Cissy went back to London without seeing Felicia.

Inevitably, the press got wind of the Gizycki cop-and-robber shenanigans. COUNT KIDNAPS BABY! said headlines around the world. Cissy's brother Joe gave a blunt interview in which he called his brother-in-law a drunk, an adulterer, a blackmailer, and a baby snatcher. The publicity provoked Gizy to ask for a million dollars in damages.

Cissy's father, who had recently had a nervous breakdown, left his sickbed to go to Europe and negotiate on her behalf. He spent the better part of a year in Vienna and St. Petersburg, attempting to work out some settlement with Gizy's lawyer, known as one of the wiliest legal minds in Austria. "Gizy seems to be a born liar," Mr. Patterson concluded, "and as for Cissy, I fear that she has tied herself into a double bow knot."

Cissy's Aunt Kate McCormick, seeing a chance to further her husband's diplomatic career, offered to help settle the family misfortune for a price. Though he was, harried, Cissy's father was not about to bargain with Kate, who had made his life at the *Tribune* miserable. He wrote to William Howard Taft, the incoming Republican

President: "Mrs. Robert McCormick has formally proposed to my wife to help my daughter with the Russian government in some of her domestic troubles, if I will agree in writing to assist McCormick get another ambassadorship. The suggestion is also that if I don't support her for an ambassadorship, she will oppose my daughter at the court of Russia."

For some five pages Patterson listed his objections to another appointment for McCormick, who he said had done little to deserve such a distinction. Moreover, Patterson charged the McCormicks with obtaining the original appointment to the Russian court by misrepresenting themselves as chief owners of the *Tribune*. To set Taft straight Patterson reported that the newspaper's stock was in the hands of trustees, of which he was one. Mrs. McCormick, Patterson pointedly declared, did not control or vote any of the stock.

Made aware of the real seat of family power, Taft threw his considerable bulk into the struggle to wrest Felicia from Count Gizycki, without installing McCormick in another diplomatic post. Taft wrote Czar Nicholas, who issued an imperial decree ordering that Felicia be returned to her mother forthwith. Count Gizycki released Felicia from her hiding place in a remote Austrian convent in August, 1909.

He took solace in claiming to the press that the Pattersons had defrauded him by false documents purporting to bear the Czar's signature. As for the $200,000 financial settlement his lawyer was able to secure, it proved insufficient to stave off creditors, and he eventually sold Cissy's silver and linen along with his estates in Novasilicia and Odessa. Even with the major issues settled, incredible legal complexities kept the Gizyckis' divorce pending and thus in the news until 1917. Cissy did not want to return to America. But, having regained possession of the child, she recognized that it would look better if she went. Otherwise she would never get off the front pages. Medill McCormick and his wife, Ruth, sailed home with her in August, 1909, and ran interference with reporters. "Now that I have my baby again, I am happy," she told the press delegation in New York. Then she boarded the train for Chicago.

"The Countess is tall and still girlish in appearance," said the Associated Press, "though her eyes bear a look of sadness that is relieved only when she smiles."

3

America Über Alles

Both branches of the *Tribune* family were disillusioned with Europeans even before the Great War. The Pattersons smarted from the Gizycki debacle, the McCormicks from the ruin of their diplomatic ambitions. All his life Bert McCormick would nurse a grudge against the British Foreign Office, which he blamed for wrecking his father's ambassadorial career by undermining his position at the Russian court.

With their biases set, the proprietors of the *Tribune**
could find little positive to say about the armed conflict which broke out in 1914. Where other commentators saw a clash of principles, the *Tribune* found only a contest between imperial ambitions.

The *Tribune* was certain of one thing—the only sane position for America was neutrality. It preached that message with vigor and went so far as to attempt to right

* Medill McCormick had suffered a nervous breakdown in 1910 and resigned from the *Tribune,* making way for joint management by Bert McCormick and Joe Patterson.

the balance when it spied pro-British sentiments building up in the United States. Thus, bucking the tide provoked charges that the Pattersons and McCormicks were pro-German and no amount of protestation ever fully cleared the tribal name, even after two family heads achieved significant war records.

Cissy invited gossip by continuing her long-standing flirtation with Count Johann von Bernstorff, the German Ambassador to the United States since 1908. The Count was greatly popular with Washington hostesses in the prewar years, when things German were the rage in America. He had a military bearing and a red mustache, and epitomized the glamour of the Kaiser's empire. Bernstorff danced divinely, the ladies said, and never let marriage stand in the way of a flirtation. As a diplomat, Bernstorff was an unusual German for the times—tactful, realistic, and an advocate of negotiations. He worked ceaselessly to stiffen Woodrow Wilson's resolve to act as a peacemaker, and at the same time tried to convince his government that American intervention on the Allied side would mean certain German defeat.

Despite this, Bernstorff's popularity declined, except with Cissy. The two continued to see each other often and once flew together in an airplane to Chicago. Rumors about their relationship reached ludicruous proportions. People said Cissy gave Bernstorff access to *Tribune* columns and insinuated that she was involved in espionage. The damaging speculation had as much truth to it as certain exaggerated accounts of German atrocities in Belgium, and it had in part the same source—the expert British propaganda fed to the United States. In McCormick's eyes the British Foreign Office was again responsible for besmirching his family name.

Bernstorff was discredited and asked to leave the United States after the British disclosed that the notorious "Zimmermann telegram" had been relayed through the German Embassy in Washington. Bernstorff apparently thought little of Foreign Minister Arthur Zimmermann's attempt to interest Mexico in a spoils alliance against America but he had followed orders. Not even Cissy defended the Count when the British disclosed that they had intercepted the cable on its way from Europe to Mexico via Washington.

Meanwhile, brother Joe and cousin Bert were touring the battlefronts and filing reports which did little to quiet pro-German attacks on the family. McCormick visited the Western Front and then, as a "distinguished foreigner," toured the Russian positions in the East under the sponsorship of Grand Duke Nicholas Nicolaevich, commander-in-chief of the Russian armies. In his files, and in a memoir, *With the Russian Army,* McCormick praised the Russian spirit but coolly assessed the Czar's military inadequacy compared to Germany's. For his part, Patterson rushed to Berlin when the war was barely three weeks old and later visited the British and French command posts. His allegiances were quickly suspect; so much so that in 1914 he was arrested by the Allies in Antwerp on suspicion of spying and was released only after the intercession of Lord Northcliffe, his English publishing friend.

Part of Patterson's trouble stemmed from his admiration of Germany's welfare-state provisions, which were begun in Bismarck's time and were without equal.

At the very least, it was an inopportune time to crow about the humanity of the Prussian state's domestic affairs. But Patterson, recognizing much that he had advocated as a young socialist, could not resist telling his home-town readers that "there aren't as many slum dwellings in all Germany as in Chicago alone."

Patterson was also impressed with the German army. He sent home chilling descriptions of its size and power.

In 1915 after inspecting the Allied Front, Patterson summed up his observations on the combatants in six lengthy articles for the *Tribune,* which were later reprinted as a book, *Notebook of a Neutral* in which he advocated American neutrality regardless of the outcome. There was simply no American interest to be served, Patterson said, by engaging in the war. He counseled isolationism towards Europe not as a pacifist but as a militant nationalist and a believer in realpolitik. He was, for example, one of the first bell ringers against the "Yellow Peril" in the Pacific.

When the United States entered the war, the *Tribune* ceased its opposition to Wilson for the duration. McCormick and Patterson, both in their late thirties, volunteered for military service. McCormick ended the war as a field artillery colonel in the First Division. He was under fire for part of the time but as far as military records show, he did not participate in any major offensives. In fact, McCormick was on sick leave during the great battle of Cantigny, for which he later named his farm in Wheaton, Illinois.* Patterson, thirty-eight and the father of three girls, was made a second lieutenant in Battery B, 149th Field Artillery, 42nd (Rainbow) Division. He was

---

* The farm was the original homestead of Joseph Medill, known as Red Oaks. During McCormick's childhood it sat at the edge of trackless prairie. He rebuilt it with English parks, a military mall and a portico modeled after Monticello.

soon promoted to first lieutenant, shipped to France in
October of 1917, and was sent into action three months
later. For fourteen weeks Patterson was under fire, participating in the second battle of the Marne, the battles of
St. Mihiel, the Argonne Forest, Champagne, and sorties
in Lorraine. He emerged a major, with a slight wound, a
taste of gas, and the affectionate nickname "Aunty Joe"
from his troops.

Their military experiences, as different as night and
day, were of elemental importance to McCormick and
Patterson; both of whom were addressed by their service
titles throughout life. Colonel McCormick spent considerable time and effort memorializing the deeds of the First
Division, even leaving his farm as a museum for the
division's military trophies. Captain Patterson confided to
a friend twenty-three years later, when the United States
was entering another war he bitterly opposed, that his
deepest desire was to drill cavalry troops. He was in his
sixties at the time.

When the war ended in 1918, the *Tribune* picked up
where it had left off in 1914. It criticized Wilson's foreign
policy and held him responsible for involving America
needlessly in what it considered a European territorial
dispute. But the *Tribune* most scorned Wilson's interna-
tionalist idealism which threatened to keep the United
States embroiled. The cynical bargaining at the peace conference confirmed the *Tribune*'s low opinions of European
statesmen and heightened its conviction that the proposed
League of Nations was folly.

The League idea was little more than a speechmaker's
generalization to the public during the Versailles Conference. Few actual details of how an international organi-

zation would work leaked out from the secret conference sessions. It was Wilson's strategy to offer the League concept to the Senate in an eloquent presentation that would galvanize public opinion. He was going to storm the isolationist barricades in "the world's most exclusive club." The President's carefully laid plans crumbled on June 9, when the *Tribune* published excerpts of the peace treaty in what remains journalism's most sensational scoop. The next morning Senator Borah had a text of the full treaty printed in the *Congressional Record*. It was a precautionary move in case the Justice Department was tempted to try the paper for breaching wartime censorship laws. The *New York Times* followed with an eight-page section, carrying the full seventy-five-thousand-word draft treaty.

Wilson, enraged and profoundly depressed, was unable to return home until three weeks later. By that time the field was held by anti-League politicians, led by Senators Lodge, Borah, Johnson, and Cissy's cousin, Medill McCormick, elected to the Senate in 1919. All hopes for Senate approval of the League faded with the President's physical collapse in September.

How the *Tribune* obtained a copy of the treaty draft may never be known. For years the mechanics of the affair were an office secret. But in 1947, in a centennial issue, the *Tribune* credited the scoop to Spearman Lewis, who had been editor of the *Tribune*'s Paris-based army edition. Lewis, according to other accounts, obtained the 416-page draft from a disenchanted member of the Chinese delegation. *Tribune* reporter Frazier Hunt then flew with the text back to Washington, where he filed the story.

Proponents of the League and of U.S. participation

excoriated the *Tribune* for a grave national disservice. Two decades later, when President Roosevelt was fighting virtually the same battle with the *Tribune,* he bitterly recalled the treaty story as the one which "broke Woodrow Wilson's heart."

Patterson and McCormick stoutly defended their professional duty to inform the public fully. Patterson's automatic reaction to critics was to accuse them of intellectualism—a disease of the mind which rendered its victims indecisive and misguided. McCormick shared his cousin's disdain for intellectuals and one of his common epithets for critics was "word men."

Furthermore, the cousins were rigid in their convictions about what was right for America. Patterson had laid the foundation of their attitude in *Notebook of a Neutral.* The realpolitik doctrine of selfish isolationism was accepted and later embellished by McCormick and Cissy.* In *The Army of 1918* the Colonel blamed Europe's troubles on the aristocratic caste which ran the courts, foreign offices and military officers' corps without any form of popular check. The lesson to America was clear: never allow power to concentrate beyond the immediate reach of the people. In one of her novels Cissy demonstrated how well she had learned the lesson at her brother's knee.

"Americans would like to aid the Old World," one of

---

* There is no clearer evidence of the *Tribune* family's steadfastness than the 1942 reprinting of *Notebook of a Neutral,* complete and without change, in their three newspapers—McCormick's *Tribune,* Patterson's *New York Daily News,* and Cissy's *Washington Times-Herald.* The *Tribune* announced the end of World War II with a front-page make up virtually similar to that of 1918, including a headline GREAT WAR ENDS.

her characters recites, "but Europe's militaristic and imperialistic policy since the Armistice has diminished our hope and destroyed our faith. Europe has greater military forces than she had before the war. Such policy is, to the last degree, brutal and stupid. And the result is that the public debt has been augmented, taxes have increased, and human misery is on the increase year after year. While the people of Europe are praying on their knees for peace, their governments are preparing for war. We will not give our help to any project of new imperialism and expansion, and in the last analysis, we will never renounce our liberty of political action, whatever talk may be going around, League of Nations or no League of Nations, World Court or no World Court."

Replaying the great issues in fiction was pale fare compared to going to war. Cissy regretted that she wasn't able to join the men in her family. During the war years she spent her time in Lake Forest, Washington, and Newport, Rhode Island. Her tedious divorce proceedings dragged on; she was restless and troublesome. Her daughter remembers her leaning back on a sofa cushion and remarking, with a flutter of fingers, "life is a series of boredoms." She virtually ignored her daughter, so that Felicia's childhood was even drearier and more isolated than Cissy's own. To protect against another kidnaping, Felicia had an armed guard as well as a governess. Arthur Meeker remembered in his book, *Chicago With Love*, why Felicia did not easily make friends. "When we played hide and seek, the game lacked *entrain* as a detective had to hide with Felicia."

During these years, Cissy lived in a kind of limbo. Her excess energy turned in on itself. Her nerves were edgy and under family prodding she came to think of herself as frail and sickly. She let doctors put her to bed for unnamed ills and she grew weak on milk diets. She joined the Aldis Players, an accomplished amateur troupe. Her mother voiced the common opinion: "I think Cissy had better not try any more theatricals. She is not calm enough to go through with it and seems paralyzed by stage fright." Although trapped in this mistaken identity, Cissy managed to build a modest reputation as an actress, with an interesting stage presence and a flair for gesture. One of her starring roles was in an early and rather bombastic socialist play, *Byproducts,* written by her brother Joe before he returned to the *Tribune.*

While keeping her house in Lake Forest, Cissy began to spend more time in Washington, which had become especially gay and exciting after 1914. Famous statesmen arrived in rapid succession and there were magnificent missions headed by such personalities as Marshal Joffre of France. Dinners and elaborate receptions and dances continued throughout the war and the hectic days of debate over the League of Nations.

Cissy went to Newport in the summer of 1914 with the Medill McCormicks, then leading figures in the Republican Party. They rented a yacht and a huge cottage on the glittering Rhode Island shore. It was a season to remember. Mrs. Stuyvesant Fish gave a ball at Newport that eclipsed all lesser glories—gold service for one hundred guests. Cissy's friend Ethel Barrymore recalled in her memoirs: "the summer in which the First World War exploded seems now to have been unlike any later summer that the world has ever known or can every know again. A summer of peace and leisure and decency, while life still moved afoot, unhurrying, when tomorrow, or the next day or the next was soon enough for the news, when the sky, all the way to the stars, was clean and still."

Cissy returned to Newport in 1915 and 1916, but was increasingly restless in society. Everywhere she went her mother and her Aunt Kate followed, bellowing advice. Since the Gizycki debacle, Cissy's mother had been as omnipresent as a governess. Mamma took over Cissy's life, hired her lawyers and servants, paid the bills, supervised Felicia's nursery, and, worst of all, spied on Cissy's love life, even bribing servants to report Cissy's callers. One afternoon, Cissy drove a pony cart through astonished guests at one of her mother's garden parties and, ripping a string of pearls from her neck she threw them in her mother's face. The necklace was a recent gift from Mrs. Patterson. But violent scenes failed to deter Mamma, and by 1916 Cissy was told by doctors she was close to a nervous breakdown. She decided to search for peace and privacy in the Wild West. Mamma was petrified of horses and too stout to risk the high altitudes in the rugged, northwestern corner of Wyoming.

4

Cissy and Cal

Joe Patterson had spent a year between Groton and Yale roving around the Western frontier. The Wild West was just Joe's meat; he liked to "rough it" and he preferred the company of rough men to any other company he knew. But he would not have expected Cissy, his silken sister, to share his enthusiasm.

Nevertheless, at age thirty-five Cissy who had always traveled with silk sheets became a convert to sheet blankets. She fell in love with the Jackson Hole Valley and the Teton country and she went so native that she wore buckskin. Cissy became one of the best female marksmen in the Northwest. She bought a hunting camp a day's horseback ride from town and lived up there for weeks at a time, riding down to Jackson Hole only when she needed bathing. As her mentor in the mountains, she adopted an extraordinary character named Cal Carrington, who was, by his own confession, an outlaw. Whenever he and Cissy walked down the main street of Jackson, people pointed to them: "There goes old Cal and the Countess."

Cissy was not the first traveler to be seduced by the Jackson Hole country. The first converts were wild animals and nomadic Indians who found the pastures rich, the winters sheltered, and the water holes deep. Then a lonely French trapper wandered by and gave a name to the valley's three heroic peaks: he christened them the Tetons because they reminded him of the breasts of beautiful women. The Jackson Hole Valley is shaped like a swooping bird, with its tail up on the Continental Divide and its beak pointing down around the Teton Pass, through which the Snake River, gorged by mountain creeks, escapes into Idaho toward the Pacific Ocean. Most of the year the valley is white with snow, but in June it is tender green, in July and August it looks blue and beige, and in mid-September patches of aspen and poplars and cottonwood light the mountainsides on fire.

It was on a late August afternoon in 1916 that Cissy first stepped off the Snake River scow into the valley, dressed in a long skirt and a veiled hat, and shivering with fatigue as Wyoming's famous clear skies cracked open and soaked her to the skin. It seemed at first that Countess Gizycka was too tender for dude ranching She took the six-day trek from Chicago in bad grace, claiming that if four dirty days on the train to Victor, Idaho, were not enough to put her in the hospital two days bouncing over the Teton Pass in a buckboard certainly were. She had carted along eleven-year-old Felicia who, without a nurse for the first time in her life, was in depressingly high spirits, and she had also brought her current French maid, Abigail, who whimpered repeatedly that she was "not accustomed" to such savage conditions. The Bar B C

Ranch, where Cissy expected to find creature comforts (because after all the place was owned by Katherine and Struthers Burt), turned out to be a cluster of primitive log cabins and tents: no plumbing, no heating, no electricity; just chamber pots, Franklin stoves, and kerosene lamps.

If it hadn't been for Abigail, the lady's maid, Cissy would have carried through on her intention to leave by the next buckboard, but when Abigail burst into tears at the prospect of washing Cissy's fine linen in an irrigation ditch, Cissy said, "Very well, Abigail, you may go home at once and take my six wardrobe trunks with you." After that Cissy felt obliged to stay.

Maximilian Struthers Burt, a distinguished man of letters as well as a dude rancher, wrote that Cissy's decision exemplified "the splendid rule of human perversity." Burt, with a Princeton education and Philadelphia newspaper experience, was one of the most articulate spokesmen for the neoromantic philosophy of the Old West—a philosophy which sentimentalized Jean-Jacques Rousseau's contention that savagery, being akin to nature, is more noble than civilization.

Throughout her lifetime romanticism in one form or another beguiled Cissy, but never so powerfully as in Jackson Hole, where suddenly she believed in God. What else but a God had created the "delicate and precise chic" of nature, the "holy" harmony between small meadows jeweled with wild flowers and the "repellent" austerity of the Tetons? She experienced moments of transcendence in which, she said, she felt her spirit, as if in a sheet of white flame, yielding itself to its maker.

"I do not deduce these rules [that there is a God]

from the principles of a high philosophy," as Rousseau wrote in *The Confessions of Faith,* "but I find them in the depths of my heart, written by nature in ineffacable characters." It was an elk-hunting expedition into the Tetons which fully converted Cissy. She recovered her vitality in a remarkably short time at the Bar B C, and insisted upon climbing into the mountains. Over the objections of Struthers Burt, Cissy persuaded Cal Carrington, the ranch's guide, to cancel his commitment to another dude and take her instead. For twenty-two days they hunted out of a permanent camp at Soda Creek, above Lake Moran, riding all day and sleeping in a leaky tent at night, until Cissy finally shot a big bull elk.

Cissy had done some shooting in Austria with Gizycki, in fact her present Mannlicher-Schoenauer rifle dated back to those days, but there she had found it poor sport —too little danger for the people, not enough chance for the animals. After three exhausting weeks chasing an elk up ravines and through down timber, however, she became as bloodthirsty as a bird dog. When at last she got a shot at the bull, she felt her heart turn over and lie still. "It's sort of a passion that comes over me," as she later described her emotion. "It isn't exactly a passion to kill, either—though maybe it is that. It comes down, I suppose, from the days when our ancestors met each other in the wild and it was constantly a matter of life and death between them."

If anyone obeyed the laws of his own nature, it was silent Cal Carrington, the guide. Cal had spent some fifty years (he did not know how old he was) unrestricted by human institutions. Abandoned as a small boy by his mother, a Swedish immigrant, he served as an apprentice to cattle rustlers and lived with Indian tribes until he staked out a couple of homesteads and hid stolen horses there. He was christened Calvin Enoch Carrington but spelled his middle name Eunuch because he thought it sounded better. He was in San Francisco during the earthquake, and he had seen the inside of a jail, but he had never stayed in one place long. He once escaped a posse by plunging his horse into the ice-swollen Snake River, and as he clung to his horse's tail for dear life, he shouted to the sheriff, "Swim it, you s— — —!"

Along with the other dudes, Cissy thought Cal was splendidly dangerous, a picture postcard of a cowboy. He was tall and divinely grizzled, bow-legged and barrel-chested, and he swung in and out of a saddle with the grace of an Indian. Easterners photographed him to prove to their friends back home that the frontier still existed. Cissy said he reminded her of a wolf—lone, savage, quick on his feet—and she started out trying to make him a pet.

Though nearly illiterate, Cal was nobody's fool. Instead of pandering to Countess Cissy he bluntly told her to look sharp and do her share of work around the camp and to stop getting in his way. He criticized the way she handled a gun. He grumbled when she said she was exhausted. Cussedness in a handsome man always stimulated Cissy's imagination, and Cal's perversity especially intrigued her because, in the mountains at least, she literally depended upon him. At times, he frightened her, and to her delight she found herself working for his approval.

Cal disliked the human race but once he got the idea that Cissy respected him, he made her an exception. He liked to watch her brushing out her long red hair and listen to her reading aloud passages from *War and Peace* by the light of the campfire. She seemed vulnerable and he felt he should protect her. When Cissy said she was going to come back to Wyoming next summer and rent a ranch, Cal said he had better manage the place for her or she would get into trouble.

Jackson buzzed with gossip that Cal Carrington was mixed up with a red-headed countess. The town got its first look at the Countess when she checked into Ma Reed's Hotel to wash off some of the dirt she had accumulated in the mountains. Jackson, in 1916, was still a frontier town with a boardwalk and hitching posts in front of the saloons and the general store, and on Saturday nights no one could sleep because of the fighting and singing and clomping of boots. Cissy, who had been dreaming about how it would feel to sleep in a real bed again after weeks in the mountains, was in a nasty mood when she came down in the morning and ran into Ma Reed, known as Jackson's toughest woman. Ma demanded a dollar from Cissy because Felicia had wet the bed. Cissy replied that in long experience with hostelries she never had seen such a poor excuse for an inn. She refused to pay so much as a dime. After a free debate, Ma said, "Git out," and shoved Cissy into the street.

It was the next summer, while Cissy was renting the White Grass Ranch, that Cal took her on a ride to his homestead on Flat Creek under Sheep Mountain. A beautiful ride on a summer morning—a long lope across the sage flats and then the climb through the timber up Cache Creek gorge. The light in the forest was like the glow of a grotto. The trail faded away, and the footing became perilous on the slippery rocks and wet grass. As

Cissy and Cal zigzagged upward, Indian style, a thin scent of snow chilled the atmosphere. Cal's cabin stood in the middle of a steep open meadow dappled with wildflowers. He pointed down the gorge and explained that he had chosen the site because any sheriff who tried to ride up there would make an easy target. Cissy thought it the most perfect place she had ever seen. Later she handed Cal a check, saying, "This is for the ranch, now you take it and shut up." He did.

A local carpenter built for her a main lodge of hewn logs with a cobblestone fireplace, a bedroom cabin on a little rocky pine-covered rise which faced upstream, a bridge across the creek, a cookhouse, a bunkhouse, a guest cabin, a corral, and, romantically, a little barn like those in Illinois. Because the site was snowed in from November through June and because every time the carpenter, Henry Crabtree, ran out of nails he had to spend a day riding down to Jackson for them, the construction went on for several years. The beauty of the camp, when he finished, was that it looked as primitive as a trapper's cabin. The cluster of dwellings cropped out of the meadow like weathered boulders and did not intrude upon the mountainside.

Cissy planned the camp as a base for hunting expeditions and a place where she could write short stories and possibly novels. She wanted it to be comfortable. Such conveniences as plumbing and electricity were out of the question; there was no plumbing even in the valley and only recently had the town of Jackson acquired electricity. Cissy made peace with outhouses, but she refused to go on hanging her clothes on rusty nails and sitting on chairs laced together with rawhide. She had furnishings shipped from the East, including a six-foot leather sofa, and a massive mahogany desk. The enormous pieces are still there. Nobody knows how to get them down the canyon or how they were taken up in the first place.

A serious servant problem faced Cissy when she set up housekeeping on Flat Creek. In the egalitarian society of Jackson Hole there were no servants, only hired girls, who called you by your first name and ate at the table with you. Despite her experience with Abigail, the lady's maid, Cissy persisted in importing Eastern domestics. One poor maid had to be tied in a saddle and hauled whimpering up the gorge. Eventually in Washington, Cissy found an adventurous young Swedish girl who could cook wild game, fend off the bears in the garbage dump, and put up with Cal's perversities.

Cal was hard on the help, especially on the hired boys. Cissy teased him about it.

"I can't find my new knife," he once said to Cissy.

"You stuck it in the new hired boy and forgot to take it out," she replied.

Cal not only harassed the help but expressed resentment against Cissy's male guests. There was nothing subtle about his sabotage techniques. He openly mocked Cissy's suitors, mounted them on dangerous horses, spat contemptuously when they tried to shoot, and made slighting references to their virility. Cissy, of course, deliberately exposed her admirers to Cal's jealousy. When Cal's tricks went too far and she chastised him, he was liable to disappear for a month. But he always came back when the hunting was good. Neither he nor Cissy hunted by the calendar. Government regulations to the contrary, they considered one season as good as another. Cal maintained that the government had no business telling a man what to do in his own mountains.

Although Cissy admitted that an old lady nearly forty ought to have better sense than to leave a comfortable camp and drag her bones around the cliffs, she said that, like Ahab, she was obsessed.

Cissy's appetite took her over Idaho's Salmon River rapids in a canoe, the first woman to make the trip, and up into the Canadian Rockies after sheep, goat, and bear. She and Cal—"the famous hunters from Jackson Hole"— traveled a regular circuit along the spine of the Rockies from British Columbia down to the west gate of Yellowstone Park. Cissy admitted that it almost killed her everytime. "Sleeping in the dirt and *snow* and dragging around those mountain peaks when I scarcely had strength to put one foot in front of another!"

It was not necessary to pursue the elusive mountain sheep into Canada. In Cissy's day vast herds of them inhabitated the windblown precipices of her own Sheep Mountain. It was, however, difficult to get a shot at one. The famous hunters would pack out of Flat Creek, taking a cook and provisions, and ride as far up the slippery slopes as the horses could keep their footing, where the hunters could set up a primitive camp. Then they would shoulder their rifles and pick their way up the rocky incline on foot, watching out for slides. The wind at these altitudes blew climbers off balance; the cold numbed their hands. In an article she wrote for *Field & Stream* Magazine, Cissy described one of the conversations she had with Cal while climbing:

HE: "My goodness, girl! Don't pick on them brambles to hang onto. You'll get all tore up."

[63]

SHE: "I'd rather hang onto a rattlesnake than bounce for a mile till I hit the bottom."

HE: "You may get a chance to. They're plenty of these suckers layin' around in that shale."

Cal's "conceit" about mountain matters maddened Cissy. She hated at any time to be told what to do, but especially when she was leaning against a sharp rock, trying to aim her rifle, with the ground slipping out from under her feet. She said it was a mercy she did not plug Cal in the head when he "jawed directions" like that. It consoled her that even Cal missed many of his shots at the sheep. With their keen eyes (as farsighted as a ten-power rifle scope) the animals usually spotted a hunter moving up the mountainside or, failing that, they skittered vertically out of range at the first crack of a gun.

Cissy followed Cal all over Sheep Mountain, tracking wounded animals and climbing down crevices after tumbled carcasses, until she became its second greatest white expert. She was proud of her performance and looked down upon weaker mortals, not only her Eastern guests but also the citizens of Jackson, who could not keep up with her on the trail of a ram. The experience of hunting goats in British Columbia, however, brought her a little closer to humility. "Goat hunting," she decided, "is not a woman's sport. To begin with, a goat hunter should be a man. And he should be young and vigorous. . . ." She made this observation after an expedition in the fall of 1920 which brought on a winter of pneumonia.

It was the element of gambling in big-game hunting which fascinated Cissy, the fact that no two shots were ever alike. "In the last analysis," she added, "what greater result can one hope for, particularly a woman, than the approval of a guide who knows work with a rifle when he observes it?" Like any cowboy Cissy looked forward to town on a Saturday night for a hot bath, a good meal, and a little celebrating in the bars. The revenue men from Denver tried occasionally to enforce prohibition in Jackson, to no avail. Stills sprouted in the mountains and the bars only shut down if someone spotted a federal agent coming down the road. Jackson was a wide-open town and proud of it. It sported blackjack, poker, dancing to fast fiddles, and plenty of brawls. As in the good old days before government.

Cissy got to know most of the people in Jackson—and she made at least one real friend in the carpenter's wife, Rose Crabtree. Mrs. Crabtree acquired a national press in 1920 by running against her husband for election to the town council and beating him. She campaigned on the cemetery ticket, claiming it scandalous that Jackson had no road to its burial ground. Henry Crabtree did not begrudge his wife the victory. Government, he agreed, was a woman's job, like housecleaning.

Wife, mother, and politician, Rose was also a full-time innkeeper. She went into the hotel business the day in 1917 that old Ma Reed asked her to look after Reed's lodgings for three weeks while Ma took a vacation. Three weeks went by and no sign of Ma; seven years went by and still no sign of Ma. Jackson Hole later learned that Ma owed $10,000 to the bank, so for all intents and purposes the Reed Hotel became the Crabtree Hotel.

Rose said she found it downright comical that she, who grew up wild and barefoot in Nebraska, should become so friendly with a titled millionairess who had grown up in a "palace." Cissy saw the irony in the situation but pointed out that they both descended from Irish peat farmers, and that as mean, tough, shanty-Irish bitches they were sisters under the skin. They addressed one another as "dear" and enjoyed being together as much as little girls in the first flush of best-friendship.

Cissy had never had a plain housewife for a friend before, and she was fascinated. Sitting in the hotel kitchen, earnestly helping Rose peel potatoes and pluck chickens, Cissy recalled her early days when kitchen meant a place of refuge from her mother and from the big hostile rooms. Since then, possessive cooks and force of habit had kept Cissy out of kitchens. In Rose's kitchen she felt like a small child again, safe and warm.

Cissy told Rose she should be grateful to have a good husband like Henry because life without a husband was awfully lonesome. She admitted that she still missed Gizy while insisting that she hated him. Rose listened to enough Gizy stories to get the impression that many of Cissy's problems with Felicia were caused by the child's resemblance to her father. Rose, who was a maternal woman, felt sorry for Felicia. But not even Rose could make Cissy into a mother. It was obvious that from the excruciating pain of childbirth until now, motherhood repelled her.

Presently Cissy announced her intention to write a short story about a love affair between characters based on her brother Joe and Rose. Since her school days she had been weaving fantasies about Joe's love life, casting friends in the role of heroine: at Farmington, Ruth Hanna; in Washington, Marguerite Cassini; in Poland, Helene Potocka. Nothing said more about Cissy's feelings than that she included Rose on her imaginary list for Joe.

George Bernard Shaw said that an Irishman's heart is nothing but his imagination. In one sense Cissy's love affair with the West was make-believe. There she was, dressed up in woolly chaps and a slouch hat, using words like "doggone" and "ain't," trying to be "just folks" with Cal and Rose while putting them both on her payroll and showering them with presents. For all her proficiency with guns and horses she never understood what it meant to live in Jackson. Her hands were not calloused. When the interminable winters set in, she went back East to have new dresses fitted and collect dividend checks.

In another sense Cissy found her real self in the West: a vigorous, earthy, aggressive woman who thrived on hard exercise and simple challenges. She discovered that after all she was not helpless.

5

The Green Hat Years

Cissy's newspaper career began in 1920 with a bit of mischief, which was how she usually got started on things. This time she put a little burr under her brother's saddle.

The *Chicago Tribune*, jointly managed by Captain Patterson and Colonel McCormick since 1910, was in a hell-for-leather competition with William Randolph Hearst's *Herald-Examiner*. In 1900 Hearst had predicted that he would have to shoot his way into Chicago, and he was right. His entrance into Chicago journalism set off the notorious circulation war which is known to have killed at least twenty-seven newsdealers, injured hundreds, and spawned future leaders of the Chicago crime Syndicate.

Fueling the Hearst-*Tribune* feud was a personal grudge of Hearst's editor, Walter Howey, against Joe Patterson. Howey had worked under Patterson as the *Tribune*'s city editor. In 1917 Patterson printed an apology on the *Tribune* editorial page for a piece of Howey's editorial judgment, and Howey went over to the opposition, where he carried out his vendetta against Patterson with a series of pranks and deadline battles.*

Perhaps it was to get her brother's attention that Cissy "treached" the *Tribune* by fraternizing with Walter Howey. Or perhaps she simply admired the fastest gun in shoot-'em-up newspapering. In any case Cissy let Walter Howey convince her to cover the 1920 Republican Convention in Chicago as a *Herald-Examiner* reporter, and she even allowed Howey to promote the news that Captain Patterson's sister was working for Hearst. Cissy's Aunt Kate McCormick, speaking for the whole family, announced in a booming voice at a Lake Forest lunch party that Hearst would rue the day he hired Cissy; certainly the *Tribune* would make no such mistake.

The man who most relished the escapade was Hearst's chief editorial executive and columnist, Arthur Brisbane. Brisbane was a great friend of the Patterson-McCormick clan even though he had been the sly intelligence behind Hearst's Chicago ventures. He was fascinated by the *Tribune* family and especially by Captain Patterson, whom he teasingly called JOMP the Cave Man. A devoted if cynical student of human behavior, Brisbane enjoyed tiffs and practical jokes; that is one reason he enjoyed Cissy. It was Brisbane who arranged for Cissy to stay in Hearst's rented house during the convention.

Hearst, as usual, was trying to arrange the affairs of the nation. He had not quieted his own ambition for the White House, but for the present he was working through another candidate—the progressive Senator Hiram John-

---

* The *Herald-Examiner* office inspired Charles MacArthur and Ben Hecht to write their famous play *Front Page*. The prototype of the editor in that play was Walter Howey.

son from California, an impressive outgrowth of Hearst's pocket.

Cissy already had earned Hearst's gratitude by campaigning with Johnson in the spring primaries, after the second defeat in the Senate of the League of Nations. Cissy toured California in Johnson's ramshackle automobile, introducing him proudly to crowds along the roadside as one "who does not believe in tying the United States up in secret with foreign diplomats who, up to date, seem to be a great deal smarter than we are." All the Republican hopefuls except Herbert Hoover were riding on the country's isolationist reaction to the traumatic war.

Coming out of the primaries, Hiram Johnson looked like an extremely strong candidate. He enjoyed the favor of the powerful Senator William E. Borah, who, with Senators Henry Cabot Lodge and Medill McCormick had managed the floor fight against the League. Borah himself remained a possibility for the nomination and Cissy secretly preferred him to Johnson.

Borah, whose massive virility was a regular matinée feature at the Senate, was in Washington parlance "a flirt" of Cissy's. Alice Roosevelt Longworth recalls that she and Medill McCormick teased Cissy and Borah with catcalls. Regardless of Alice's teasing, luring Senate lions was a respectable sport among Washington ladies, and Borah was a prize of prizes. But Cissy lost him during the 1920 Convention.

The Borah wrath, according to gossip in the press, was provoked by an article Cissy wrote for Hearst's *Herald-Examiner* headlined BORAH IS COUNTESS GIZYCKA'S HERO. Apparently Cissy couldn't resist showing off a little about her privileged relationship with the Idaho idol. Her prose about his leonine profile and magnetic speaking voice was embarassingly affectionate, and Borah, married and sensitive to public opinion, warned her against further indiscretion. Then, by coincidence, the *Chicago Tribune* printed an editorial criticism of Borah. It was interpreted as the fury of a woman scorned but, in fact, neither Captain Patterson nor Colonel McCormick gave Cissy a voice in editorial policy.

Whether Borah's reaction to her newspaper article was the real reason for Cissy's animosity against the Senator, she turned on him, and her feelings were scarcely soothed when Borah joined Alice Roosevelt Longworth's salon. Cissy's gratitude to the President's daughter had dissipated since their debutante days, when "Princess Alice" brought Cissy into the "Cabinet Circle". Now they were fighting like equals. One famous story about them, probably apocryphal, is that one night after a dinner party when Cissy had, as usual, vamped Mrs. Longworth's guest of honor, Mrs. Longworth sent her chauffeur to Cissy's house with a packet of hairpins and a note: "Cissy, dear, you left these under the sofa cushions." Cissy replied, "Alice, please look in the chandelier, I think you will find my garter."

Catcalls and female rivalries were entirely appropriate to the 1920 Republican Convention that Edna Ferber, who reported it, called "as poisonous a political mess as any party stirred up in the history of the United States." Hearst's candidate lost the nomination, but not to General Leonard Wood. Out of a murky suite at the Blackstone Hotel came a wisp of smoke named Warren Gamaliel Harding. "A slob," is what Mrs. Longworth called

Harding, but Evalyn Walsh McLean, Washington's richest woman, disagreed. "Whatever Alice says, I say he is not a slob," maintained Evalyn, who had recently bought the Hope Diamond to cheer herself up. Mrs. McLean managed Washington Society from her huge estate, Friendship, during the inglorious Harding Administration while her husband, Edward, advised the President as a member of the "Kitchen Cabinet." During the next three years Evalyn and Ned McLean were the unchallenged leaders of Washington Society. At about this time Cissy decided she could not stand Evalyn. It was all subject for satire, and Cissy went to Paris that autumn to write a novel.

"To A.B., W.H., and J.M.P., whose fault it was," read the dedication on Cissy's *Glass Houses*. She wrote the novel in French, and it was published in Europe in the *Revue de Paris* before it appeared in America. Dedicating a book to Arthur Brisbane, Joseph Patterson, and Walter Howey was nearly as brash as writing holes through the characters of Alice Roosevelt Longworth and Senator Borah. *Glass Houses* was written in the current vogue of jazzy sentences, descriptions of lovemaking, and enthusiastic revelation of degenerate postwar America, and the writing was admirably light. But it was a deliberately bitchy book.

The story tells of a Wyoming politician's daughter (Cissy) who pursues a long-standing love affair with a Western senator (Borah) while beginning another love affair with a French diplomat (part Gizycki, part Bernstroff), under the jealous eye of a feverish, aggressive Washington hostess (Mrs. Longworth). The senator, a thorough cad, comes to an untimely end in the mountains of Jackson Hole when the heroine's tough old cowboy-cum-governess (Cal Carrington) shoots him for playing lightly with his mistress' affections. The senator's murder frustrates the ambitions of the despicable hostess, who was bidding for his favor. The cowboy, a symbol of natural law, goes unpunished, and the lovely heroine marries the diplomat.

Cissy's writing habits were glamorous. She worked in a suite at the Paris Ritz. Since she originally submitted her efforts to the *Revue de Paris,* she collaborated with a Parisian she described as "old and homely, with only a few hairs left on his head." The collaborator became amorous and passionately ripped her "very best tea-gown." Dismissing him, she traveled to the Riviera, where she conversed with such literary lights as Somerset Maugham; later she claimed he had included her as a character in one of his stories.

The American version of *Glass Houses* appeared only after the death in 1925 of Cissy's cousin, Senator Medill McCormick,* who was a close friend of the Longworths. Her second book, *Fall Flight,* a fictionalized autobiography of the years of her marriage to Gizycki, was written after the Count's death in 1926. Cissy told a friend that on the night Gizycki died, in Vienna, he had appeared to her in a dream, dressed in shiny Peel boots. She called him "the only love of my life." In *Fall Flight,* however, she portrayed him as a sadist and her mother as a vulgarian.

Cissy's mother had suffered a heart attack in 1920 from

---

* Senator McCormick had been unsuccessful in his campaign for renomination the previous year and died, said Cissy, of a broken heart.

which she never quite recovered although she lived another thirteen years. By 1923 old Mrs. Patterson had become fuzzy-minded and too heavy for her ankles. Her children persuaded her to move into the Drake Hotel in Chicago, where she would not be bothered by "fire engines rushing around Dupont Circle." Her fortune, about $15,-000,000, was safely in the Joseph Medill Trust, and she agreed to direct the bulk of her income to her children. She agreed also that the majority of her property be divided equally between Joe and Cissy. Joe, successor to his father as trustee of the Joseph Medill Trust, was appointed arbitrator of the partition.

Captain Joe was excessively businesslike about the arrangements. He even deducted the expenses for Felicia Gizycka's debutante party from Cissy's share of the spoils. Cissy interpreted her brother's scrupulous tactics as greed, and in a letter to the trust officer at their bank she suggested that "my brother is set on making an excellent bargain for himself." The Captain's temper flared at the insinuation: "The question of $50,000," he declared, "is not worth a quarrel. I wouldn't quarrel with you for that amount and don't think you should quarrel with me. . . . It is plain you think I am trying to skin you. Well, I am not."

Joe Patterson was dismayed that his sister seemed to be turning into another Aunt Kate McCormick. He reminded her that the family had suffered cruelly from short-sighted jealousies and ferocity. Joe had "been through the mill" with Cissy. "Watch out for her," he warned his daughter, Alicia. "She'll bitch you every time." His feelings toward her were decidely ambivalent. He was proud of her, embarassed by her, afraid of her, and contemptuous of her, all at the same time. Joe and Cissy were still close—their cousin, Colonel Robert McCormick, remarked that he felt like an outsider in their company. Yet Joe manuevered to keep his distance.

The war had changed Joe Patterson. He had fought with the First Illinois Cavalry through all the principal battles in France in 1917, and despite his mother's efforts to have him transferred to a safer station, he remained with the troops until the Armistice. But in proving his courage and stamina, he had toughened more than his guts. Though still capable of surprising sweetness, he had become a professional hard-line man, impatient with people, which may have been one cause for the subsequent failure of his marriage.

The war also had rekindled Patterson's grander ambitions. Dissatisfied with his position at the *Chicago Tribune*, where he had to share the editorial page with his more conservative cousin, Joe wanted a newspaper to run his own way, and he wanted to try to crack the New York market. Captain Patterson and Colonel McCormick conferred in Europe in 1918—supposedly on a French manure pile—and decided to borrow *Tribune* money to launch *The Illustrated New York Daily News*, a tabloid modeled on Lord Northcliffe's London *Daily Mirror*. By 1921 this enterprise, published by Patterson, had become the largest morning newspaper in Manhattan, and today it is the largest newspaper in America.

Cissy hadn't contributed to the remarkable growth of the Tribune Company, whose profits had tripled since her grandfather Medill's death, yet she was complaining. With some bitterness her brother and cousin insisted that she owed only gratitude to the *Tribune*.

The only cloud on the *Tribune* horizon was the prospect of crippling inheritance taxes upon the deaths of
Elinor Patterson and Katherine McCormick—taxes which
could force the family to sell stock and lose control of the
company. Weymouth Kirkland, the *Tribune* legal expert,
devised an ingenious legal instrument, a Patterson-Mc-
McCormick Trust, created in 1932, a year before Mrs.
Patterson finally died. Into this trust the McCormicks and
Pattersons poured their once and future stock, putting
their voting control into the hands of three trustees, two
of whom were Colonel McCormick and Captain Patterson. According to the agreement Cissy was to replace her
brother if he died first. A continuation of the original
Joseph Medill Trust, it enforced discipline within the
family ranks and assured the line of succession.

The last years of the red-haired Medill sisters, Kate and
Nellie, were violent and melancholy. When Cissy went to
Chicago to visit her mother, Mrs. Patterson would beat
her cane on the floor and cry, "Joe, Joe, where's Joe?"
Irrationally frightened by the sight of her mother's ill-
ness, Cissy saw her as little as possible. Aunt Kate Mc-
Cormick was also senile but she kept her sense of humor.
When a plump friend prayed at Mrs. McCormick's bed-
side, the old lady boomed out from the deathly silence,
"*My God*, what a bottom!"

In 1923 Cissy moved into her mother's Dupont Circle
mansion, grumbling that it was "an old house in a no
longer fashionable part of town." She promptly set about
dispelling what she called "the banal perfection of great
American salons." Relegating Victorian cakestands and
red plush divans to the attic, she ripped the red velvet off
the balustrades and replaced dark Oriental rugs with gay

Aubussons. She hung her hunting trophies in the entrance hall. The house, which had been dreary and pompous, was now as gay as a movie set.

While in residence Cissy kept the four floors and thirty rooms alive with guests because it was a terrible house to live in alone. She employed a staff of ten, including footmen in green livery. In 1926, when she was spending most of her time in New York, Cissy rented Dupont Circle to Calvin Coolidge while the White House was undergoing repairs. The White House steward expressed amazement that the public rooms were so grand in comparison to the private living quarters—especially Cissy's favorite fourth-floor apartment, a separate tiny flat in the trees. Charles Lindbergh visited the Coolidges at Dupont Circle after his flight to Paris, and Cissy afterward hung a little bronze plaque in the "Lindbergh Bedroom." But the honor of being a President's landlady hardly impressed her. She was glad to see Mr. Coolidge go, she said, because he fed his dog scraps of meat on her dining-room rug.

Having grumbled for years about her "skinflint" mother and measly $10,000 annual allowance, Cissy was finally expressing her royal tastes. Walking past Cartier's window in New York, she spied a familiar string of black pearls; upon inquiring, she discovered that they belonged to Princess Irina Youssoupoff, the wife of Rasputin's assassin and the niece of the late Czar. When Pierre Cartier explained to Cissy that the Princess had not yet put a price on the pearls, which were unique, Cissy wrote out a blank check. Another one of her purchases was a little boudoir railroad car, which she outfitted with different sets of chintz for different seasons of the year and christened Ranger after her favorite Wyoming pony. Since she traveled a great deal, the Ranger proved a handy luxury, and it was a nice way to entertain friends as well as transport her servants and dogs from town to town.

But the richness of life soon seemed indigestible, and she longed for leaner youth. "I'm discouraged," she confessed. "Just by life. I can't seem to get through."

Having subsisted since girlhood on the admiration of men, she brooded over the thinning ranks of her admirers. "I find them as unappetizing as spinach," she said, referring to her current crop of beaux. When Fred McLaughlin eloped with the dancer Irene Castle, Cissy tried to dismiss them "a couple of old fools," but her pique showed. Proof to Cissy of her advancing age was that her daughter Felicia had become a beautiful and rebellious young woman. A full-bosomed blonde, Countess Felicia seemed to have nothing of her mother but a deep husky voice. And she was, naturally enough, bitter at the way her mother had neglected her. Cissy found her "about as easy to handle as a team of bull moose." At the same time that Felicia began to express her deep resentment, Cissy turned into a possessive and interfering mother. "When I reached my teens," Felicia recalls, "Mother wanted me around all the time." Felicia felt extremely uncomfortable in Cissy's presence. Cissy said sadly, "Felicia and her friends look on me as a kind but consumptive old party."

As she grew older Cissy became obsessed with the affairs of the younger generation. She enjoyed dabbling in "the love life of children." Although she made cutting remarks about Felicia's physical attractions and lied about her daughter's age in order to diminish her own years, she nevertheless encouraged young men to court Felicia.

One she particularly encouraged was a twenty-seven-year-old newspaper reporter named Drew Pearson, who had fallen in love with the eighteen-year-old countess at a Dupont Circle dinner party. Without consulting Felicia, who thought the mustached Pearson was older than God and twice as terrifying, Cissy invited him to visit them at the Flat Creek Ranch which he, who spent his whole bankroll on railroad fare to Victor, Idaho, naturally took as an indication of Countess Felicia's esteem. Pearson arrived on horseback at Flat Creek Ranch to discover himself in the middle of hostilities between mother and daughter Gizycka. Actual warfare broke out one morning when Cissy fired her lady's maid but refused the woman transportation from the ranch into town. Young Felicia accused Cissy of slaveholding. She announced that she would take the maid into town on the back of her pony. The maid, who hated horses, tearfully declined to be rescued. But Felicia departed anyway, strapping her worldly goods on her saddle.

Cissy pretended not to care that her daughter was leaving home, but as soon as the runaway rode out of sight, she dispatched the bewildered but ardent Pearson to find Felicia and bring her back. Felicia knew the trails and caught the stagecoach to Idaho before her beau reached Jackson Hole. Pearson eventually caught up with Felicia on the train to Salt Lake City, but Felicia would not speak to him. In Salt Lake she shed him and got a job as a waitress in a hash house.

Another witness to Felicia's runaway was a forty-three-year-old lawyer named Elmer Schlesinger who had been courting Cissy ever since his friend Albert Lasker brought him to Washington in 1921 as a counsel to the Shipping Board. No one expected that Cissy took Schlesinger seriously. Cissy's friends and family disapproved of him. They thought him cynical and unstable. He had recently divorced his wife, leaving her in Chicago with two adolescent children. However, for the very reasons which others found objectionable, Cissy liked Elmer Schlesinger. "I love vulgar people if they just have a little charm." Actually she loved Schlesinger because he made her feel young. They had many characteristics in common: they were both clever, intuitive and hot-tempered. Both were incurable romantics.

During the months when Countess Felicia was working incognito in Salt Lake City her mother lived in Washington and consoled herself with the company of Schlesinger and young Drew Pearson. In the spring of 1925, encouraged by Cissy and Schlesinger, Pearson traveled out West and persuaded Felicia to give up her job and elope with him.

While Washington society was adjusting to her ill-fitting role as mother of the bride, Cissy shattered the social columns with the news that she had gone to New York with Elmer Schlesinger and married him in a civil ceremony at City Hall. "I'm happier than I ever was before," she told reporters. Some of her friends thought she had gone mad. "We couldn't believe it," Mrs. Longworth recalls. Drew Pearson was the only witness at the wedding, and Cissy said later that his persuasion convinced her to go through with it. The Schlesingers sailed to Italy for their honeymoon on the sumptuous S.S. *Conte Verde*. A Washington friend ran into Cissy during the journey and attempted congratulations. "Oh, I'm not sure how this will work," Cissy replied airily. She seemed content that

she and Schlesinger were physically attracted to one another and proud that she could still kindle such desire.
She also dwelt upon her groom's business acumen, which
she took as proof that he wanted her for herself and not
for her money.

After their wedding trip the Schlesingers leased a vast
apartment at 1010 Fifth Avenue in New York, a short
limousine ride from Schlesinger's office at 120 Broadway,
where he was a partner in the law firm of Chadbourne,
Stanfield, Levy & Price. For the warm months they
bought Vincent Astor's Harbor Acres, an estate at Sands
Point, which overlooks Manhasset Bay.

After the surfeit of political exposure in Washington,
Cissy found New York Society refreshing and she entertained constantly. At one party she hired quadroon girls
to perform the "Black Bottom" dance, bare-breasted, after
dinner. She enjoyed speakeasies, slumming in Harlem,
and prize fights.

In 1926 Cissy's Paris novel came out in America. Literary columnists called it an inside view into "the bosoms of
better-known families" and hinted darkly at domestic
crises it was causing in Washington. Mrs. Longworth was
not amused, though publicly she insisted she was. Mrs.
Longworth's husband, Nicholas, the most amiable
Speaker in the history of the House of Representatives,
reluctantly feigned outrage. He promised to cut Cissy
dead, but since he and Cissy were long-time flirts and
friends, he could not go through with it. "If any man ever
caused trouble between Cissy and me, it was my husband
Nick," recalls Mrs. Longworth. "He adored her."

Cissy's literary career gave her an entrée into the glamorous Algonquin Round Table. The friends of the Round

Table gathered not only at the Algonquin Hotel but at *New Yorker* editor Harold Ross's dilapidated town house, artist Neysa McMain's studio loft, and journalist Herbert Bayard Swope's croquet field at Sands Point. Among the habitués were Harpo Marx, Joseph Pulitzer, Heywood Broun, Helen Hayes, Bernard Baruch, Jack Dempsey, Averell Harriman, George Kaufmann, and Irving Berlin. Everyone seemed to have plenty of money, the talk was good, and the atmosphere was electric but not self-conscious. Cissy and Elmer Schlesinger filtered in and out of the Algonquin Set. She was notable for her dramatic entrances, as the late arrival, dripping with diamonds and followed by five or six men, looking to younger eyes like a spoiled and ravaged courtesan, yet somehow epitomizing glamour.

Cissy's marriage to Schlesinger bloomed briefly and then withered into ugliness. Within two years, they were discussing divorce. In February of 1929 Mr. Schlesinger suddenly slumped down on the golf course at Aiken, South Carolina, where he was visiting C. Oliver Iselin at his estate, Hopelands. When she heard the news in Washington, Cissy reacted with characteristic inconsistency by bursting into hysterics. In a frenzy of remorse and self-pity she robed herself in widow's weeds and set off for Aiken in her railroad car to bring the body back to Dupont Circle for the funeral. Drew Pearson, although Felicia had divorced him, stayed by the side of his former mother-in-law and helped her arrange a large important funeral. The honorary pallbearers included four senators, two members of the Cabinet, the British Ambassador, the Speaker of the House, a brigadier general, seven tycoons, and other distinguished friends.

"I have lost my child," Cissy wrote to Rose Crabtree in Wyoming. "Every waking moment of the night I want to put my arms around him and tell him not to be frightened —that I'll take care of him."

Felicia remembers that her mother "went to pieces" after Schlesinger's death. Cissy told friends that she felt old, useless, and miserable, and that she doubted she would feel like laughing again. To escape her private furies Cissy traveled around the country in her railroad car for two months, and returned to New York more miserable than before. She flirted with psychoanalysis, but she could not take it seriously. Her profound depression explains to some degree why Cissy behaved badly about Schlesinger's estate. Elmer Schlesinger died without leaving a will, and to Cissy's surprise the Harbor Acres property, deeded in his name, descended to his two children. Cissy had paid for Harbor Acres, and she intended to keep it. In her nervous state she decided that Schlesinger had planned to rob her in favor of his children. With massive indiscretion she spread the story among their mutual friends, and then sued the Schlesinger children.

After Schlesinger's death she asked architect Raymond Hood, designer of the Tribune building, to plan an elaborate mausoleum for Schlesinger's coffin. When she learned of his will, she canceled the mausoleum plans without a word of explanation to Hood who had been living at Dupont Circle waiting for consultation. Cissy, a year later, under a cloak of secrecy, arranged that Schlesinger's body be brought to Washington again, but she did not attend the second burial.

Her husband's death left Cissy at loose ends. Felicia

left the United States for a protracted stay in Europe, taking Cissy's baby granddaughter, Ellen, with her. Cissy was left alone to ramble aimlessly across country in her private railroad car.

6

Hearstling

Cissy had run out of diversions when her old friend Arthur Brisbane wrote to her, "Come back from your gypsy wandering and start something that will be useful to the world. . . . Stop dragging your railroad car all over the country searching for sensations of superiority which you ought to get by *mental* achievement."

While married to Elmer Schlesinger, Cissy had already talked to Brisbane about getting into the newspaper business. Brisbane was one of the giants of journalism—his daily "Today" column, a collection of chatty observations on the news, reached twenty-five million readers, according to the Hearst distributing agency. Brisbane composed with phenomenal swiftness, usually dictating his column in twenty or thirty minutes after skimming late newspaper editions. For that and his services as an editor and national editorial advisor, Hearst paid him $260,000 a year. A shrewd investor and admirer of money, Brisbane amassed a $25,000,000 estate in the course of a career that began with a reporter's job on the *New York Sun* at the age of nineteen. Cissy considered him brilliant and wicked—excellent things in men. He was a Nietzsche disciple and had a contemptuous view of his mass readership. The son of a radical economist, Brisbane, like Hearst, began as an extreme liberal and worked his way back to a cantankerous, disillusioned conservatism.

Brisbane was in his sixties when he put Cissy on the search for a newspaper to buy. Tall and well-preserved, with a high forehead and steel-rimmed glasses, Brisbane appeared frosty and pompous, but he had a Voltairian wit. And he was always game for experiments. He was amused by the thought of what Cissy Patterson would do to the newspaper business and delighted with the prospect of dissension within the Patterson–McCormick family.

As early as 1928 Brisbane and Cissy approached William Randolph Hearst about selling his *Washington Herald,* a mediocre morning newspaper which consistently lost money. Hearst did not choose to sell. He wanted a morning paper to balance his evening paper in the nation's capital, a question of prestige. Besides, Hearst enjoyed amassing property, not distributing it. A man who would buy a Spanish monastery and leave it crated in a warehouse was not a man to dispose of a newspaper.

In early 1930 Brisbane tipped Cissy off that Washington's other morning newspaper, the *Post,* was coming on the market. Publisher Edward McLean III, whom Cissy had known since her debutante days and whom the country knew from his ill-advised membership in Harding's "Kitchen Cabinet," had suffered a nervous breakdown.

Cissy went to see her brother Joe and ask his advice about buying the *Post.* She considered Joe's newspaper judgment impeccable. After all, his *New York Daily News* had achieved the largest newspaper circulation in the country, 1.3 million daily, within the first ten years of its life. Brisbane moaned: "Patterson is no genius. In some ways, he isn't even smart, and we are letting him get away with this!" Cissy never said so to Brisbane, but she privately considered her brother smarter than all the "geniuses" in the Hearst organization put together.

Joe did not encourage his sister to buy the *Post*. He said she was crazy to think she could run a newspaper, especially a losing newspaper, and especially a newspaper in Washington, a city known as a publishers' graveyard. He reminded her that she lacked the most basic experience. He predicted that if she bought the *Post*, she would lose her fortune and run into debt. He doubted, furthermore, that she had the temperament for publishing.

Reluctantly Cissy kept her money in the bank, but within two months she was pestering Mr. Hearst about his *Herald* again. "Why don't you sell it to her?" Brisbane chided Hearst. "She is a very smart girl and she ought to have it. Her grandfather was a great newspaperman."

Hearst enjoyed Cissy and agreed with Brisbane that her position and reputation in Washington would enliven his *Herald*. He was sixty-seven in 1930 and, like Brisbane, he saw much of his life behind him, though he was to live another twenty-one years. His towering political ambitions, which at one time had included the Presidency, were dead. His private and public reputations were hopelessly compromised. His relationship with actress Marion Davies, however devoted, was common gossip. His editorial voice, once so influential among the masses, was compromised by years of news slanting, vendettas, and outright fabrications. In New York his *Journal, Mirror,* and *American* were being outflanked by the tabloid *Daily News* and the dignified *New York Times.**

The Depression was to do more damage to Hearst's glittering empire than his own faults of character. But in 1930 his childlike optimism blinded Hearst to the gathering whirlwind. He continued to spend more than his income on works of art, lavish living, and the construction of his California castle, San Simeon. Meanwhile, his various enterprises ran up the Hearst business debt to $110,-000,000 at the very time he should have been retrenching.

Hearst thought he had nothing to lose by experimenting with the dilapidated *Herald.* He paid as highly for names as for talent. He had once tried to hire Cornelius Vanderbilt as editor of the *New York Mirror* on the grounds that the name Vanderbilt was worth $30,000 a year. Now he wanted Eleanor Medill Patterson on the masthead of his *Washington Herald.* Hearst considered the words Medill and Patterson so important that he persuaded Cissy to go to court and remove Schlesinger from her name. No one expected Cissy to do more than lend her name to the masthead. But her greatest supporter, Brisbane, cautioned, "I hope and am not sure that you will work hard. Enjoyment is one thing, work is another.

---

* But if Hearst's fortunes were declining, they still had a long way to fall. Starting in 1887 as a twenty-four-year-old editor intent on salvaging his father's money-losing *San Francisco Examiner,* Hearst had built a communications empire of twenty-two daily papers, fifteen Sunday papers, and nine magazines, which with other investments produced his annual income of $15,000,-000.

Unless you take Dante's advice and *work in fire,* you won't pan out."

In case the experiment was a bust Hearst was ready with an exit. He was casual about hiring and firing people. *Washington Herald* editors came and left so quickly that some of the staff never learned their names; their contracts were written so the publisher could terminate the arrangement at will. Hearst executives, when they heard about Cissy, assured one another that she might last a week at the most.

Cissy's trial by fire began in July, one month after Hearst hired her for $10,000 when she left the cool lawns of her Harbor Acres estate for the steaming sidewalks of Washington. Never having spent a summer in a city, and particularly sensitive to heat, she felt immediately overworked and underpaid and was in a surly mood when she stepped out of her limousine and took her first walk into the Herald Building. She was wearing a big straw hat and she looked fierce. The *Herald* city room had been warned she might come, but the staffers were not prepared for the sight of her in the flesh, glowering at them. A few stood up and grabbed for their coats, but most of them just stared. "I suppose you think this is just a stunt!" she declared in a low withering voice. The typewriters all stopped and nobody breathed. Then she said, "Well even if you do, let's all try to put it over." She looked around at each man in turn until a smile spread imperceptibly over her lips. "I think I'm going to like this," she said, and then she swept out, leaving them to scratch their heads. If a talking seal had introduced itself as their editor, they would not have been more surprised.

Cissy's two-room office suite was dingy and without

personality when she began work. It had been little more than a nook where the many *Herald* editors had hung their hats and opened their briefcases. Cissy decorated it to suit a lady. Against one wall she put an antique table, and at another wall a leather-covered sofa and marble-topped coffee table. Four antique leather-backed and cane-seated chairs were scattered around the main office room. Family portraits, including one of Joseph Medill, were hung on the gray-pink walls. The floors were redone in hardwood parquet. Two Regency pieces and a highboy held her books. A refrigerator, hot plate, air conditioner and humidifier added comfort.

The *Herald* readers met Cissy on July 23, 1930, when a large and flattering drawing of her face, by the fashionable Neysa McMain, appeared on page one, flanked by telegrams from famous people exclaiming her "real genius" and her success as a novelist and writer. This promotion was in the same style used by Hearst papers to review Marion Davies' movies. Cissy Patterson was described not only as a great newspaperwoman and a raving beauty, but also as an ingenue, seemingly no older than twenty-nine.

Though Cissy did not quite know what an editor was supposed to do, she had a lot of ideas. Clearly, one of an editor's jobs was to write editorials. Though most editorials within his organization originated with Mr. Hearst in California—arriving prepackaged, like the columns and comics and most of the news, over a wire—Cissy thought he wouldn't mind if she wrote one small one of her own.

"When Cissy got ahold of that paper, I *knew* she'd do *something* to me," recalls Alice Roosevelt Longworth. Since the publication of *Glass Houses*, their enmity had grown ever more bitter, and Cissy was going around Washington saying she could hardly wait to hit Alice over the head with a newspaper. Cissy needed some newsworthy angle for an anti-Alice editorial and she grabbed the first one that came along, which was wise, because Mrs. Longworth generally kept her name out of the news. The exception was an announcement that Mrs. Longworth intended to manage the campaign of Ruth Hanna McCormick for the Illinois Senate seat left vacant by the death of her husband, Cissy's first cousin, Medill McCormick. When she read the announcement, Cissy scribbled some words on the back of a telephone book, then called up city editor Mike Flynn and told him to take dictation. "Put that right on the front page, in a box, signed with my name," she ordered the surprised Flynn. "Be sure it's on the front page. Mr. Hearst says that's the only place people will read it." On the morning of August 5, 1930, an astonished Washington stared at Cissy's front-page box:

Interesting But Not True

Reports that Mrs. Alice Roosevelt Longworth will manage the Senate campaign of Mrs. Ruth Hanna McCormick are interesting, but not true.

Mrs. McCormick takes no advice, political or otherwise, from Mrs. Longworth.

Mrs. Longworth could not possibly manage anyone's campaign, being too lofty to speak to newsmen and too aristocratic for public speaking.

Mrs. Longworth gives no interviews to the press.

Mrs. Longworth cannot utter in public.

Her assistance, therefore, will evolve itself as usual into posing for photographs.

ELEANOR MEDILL PATTERSON (signed)

"Very amusing," Mrs. Longworth commented with disturbing sweetness. She did not dignify Cissy's attack with a reply. Nevertheless Cissy's "little piece about Alice," as she called it, made news all over the country, and by her first act in office Cissy achieved a celebrity to which most editors never aspire. The *Herald* circulation jerked up a little and Mr. Hearst described himself as simply tickled pink. Joe Patterson thought his sister had wasted no time making a fool of herself. Captain Patterson ran a sensational tabloid, but he found Cissy's personalized attack nauseating and unprofessional. Even Arthur Brisbane objected. He had not guessed she would go so far, especially in her first week on the job. He wrote her a polite note warning against transforming the *Herald* into "a woman's paper." He reminded her that sugar tastes better than vinegar. "Scrapping with Alice is all very well," he said, "but you must keep the high *Joseph Medill* level.

Asking Cissy to be a great editor in the classic sense was like asking a fish to fly. She had never reported hard news, never worked in a newsroom, and was hardly familiar with the mechanics of getting out a newspaper. If she was going to fly at all, it had to be by the seat of her pants. She did know a few tricks—some she had picked up from her family and some she had figured out by herself—and these she meant to exploit for all they were worth. Her position as a woman editor of a major newspaper made Cissy unique in the country, and people expected her to behave oddly. She recognized this. In a radio interview she quoted Samuel Johnson on woman preachers: "Sir, a woman preaching is like a dog walking on its hind legs. It is not done well; but you are surprised to find it done at all."

When she took on the editorship of the *Herald,* Cissy found so many demands on her time that like the old woman in the shoe, she didn't know what to do, and it bothered her fragile nerves. Between working during the day and campaigning on the *Herald's* behalf during the evenings, Cissy soon wore herself out, and her temper showed the strain. While she petted and pampered some friends, she behaved like a bitch to the people who worked for her. Because the Depression was on, her employees did not quit.

During a typical day Cissy exploded half a dozen times. She usually woke up cross because she slept badly and her head ached from too much champagne the night before. The irritations began the moment she rang for her breakfast tray, usually about ten o'clock. A lukewarm piece of toast might cost somebody his job. She ate breakfast in bed, surrounded by her six poodles, the morning newspapers, and the day's mail. While the telephone rang and the dogs hopped around the bedclothes, her housekeeper and her secretary stood by with notepads, transcribing orders and begging Mrs. Patterson's attention to urgent matters. Cissy hated details like paying bills, approving menus, and checking guest lists, yet she insisted on checking every housekeeping item personally, though she got angry every time she was asked for a little decision. The resulting waste, inefficiency, and graft within her household so annoyed her that she periodically demanded sweeping reforms, all doomed to failure. She said she simply could not understand why with all the people on her staff, about fifteen, the household did not run like a jeweled watch. Neither her secretary nor her financial manager nor her housekeeper dared suggest the reason.

At about eleven-thirty Cissy would sweep out of Dupont Circle and get into her limousine, poodles at her side, to ride downtown. Her chauffeurs, when opening the car door, had to watch out for the snapping dogs; Cissy allowed them to bite people. While Cissy drove to the *Herald,* her secretary had to catch a taxi and beat the limousine, because though Cissy never offered her secretary a ride, she expected her to be waiting for her at the office. Meantime, back at the marble palace, Cissy's lady's maid spent the remainder of the morning laboriously combing through the mountain of newspapers in the bedroom, salvaging checks and documents hidden between the sports and food sections. Cissy had a habit of losing her important mail and then blaming the servants, just as she would habitually drop her jewelry behind her dressing table or under the bed and then imagined it had been stolen.

Cissy's arrival at the *Herald* inevitably produced a flurry of activity. She generated fear because no one knew what might annoy her. There was a belief at the paper that she enjoyed firing people, that she was the Red Queen shouting "Off with his head," that she drank blood for lunch. Actually she was afraid of her staff. She thought they laughed at her behind her back and wanted to take advantage of her. If, from her editor's glass cubicle off the city room, she noticed a man staring at the ceiling, she assumed that he was drunk or malingering.

Cissy did not know what standards to demand of her employees. She would call in a new reporter and say she wanted a sensational scoop for tomorrow's paper, or tell her business manager she wanted the *Herald's* circulation to hop, skip and jump upward—immediately. By asking the impossible, Cissy sometimes accomplished it, and her unorthodox methods injected great vitality into the long lifeless *Herald.* But she was making her staff nervous.

Though she brooked no familiarity—everyone in the office called her Mrs. Patterson—Cissy wanted to be liked, and she chose friends at the *Herald.* She often invited one or two people to lunch with her, either in her private office (her chef sent food down) or at Dupont Circle. During lunch she relaxed a little, drank a couple of Scotches, and seemed "as easy as an old shoe." She solicited interoffice gossip and giggled about it. Most guests at her intimate luncheons mistakenly assumed she wanted to be "one of the boys," and they favored her with confidences, which like as not she used as weapons in her arsenal. After lunch Cissy might work a few more hours —dictating correspondence, conferring with her executives, talking on the telephone—and then go home to rest before the evening. If she had no previous engagement, she often called up friends and invited them for dinner, telephoning her kitchen to prepare lobster thermidor and *crêpes suzette* for twelve, but neglecting to tell the chef how to obtain twelve lobsters before the shops closed.

Cissy's parties went on late into the night and her servants were expected to work around the clock when necessary. She paid a little higher than the average wage because the word had traveled in domestic circles that her house was a hardship post. One footman managed to stay out of her sight for six months, and when she finally noticed him, she bawled him out. She really considered her servants the enemy—so many of them and only one of her. On a full-time basis she retained a head butler, several footmen, a housekeeper, a houseman, one or two chauffeurs, a lady's maid, two laundresses, a seamstress, and a secretary. And on her three-room railroad car there were two ancient Negroes and a steward, nicknamed by Brisbane "the Czechoslovakian admiral." After staying at Dupont Circle, young Seward Brisbane told his father that three butlers attempted to tie his white cravat and when they couldn't do it, the head butler sent the two other butlers to get the head butler's tie. An efficient German lady, Mrs. Sibill Campbell, tried valiantly to oversee the staff, but Cissy made Mrs. Campbell's job almost impossible.

Though Cissy was a wanton housekeeper and a perverse administrator of her staff, her parties were the envy of social Washington. Mrs. Frank Allen West, one of the city's *grande dames*, recalled that "Cissy gave the most splendidly appointed parties. Mrs. [Evalyn Walsh] McLean gave the biggest, of course, but one was likely to find soot on the centerpiece at Friendship House, never at Dupont Circle."

Cissy served the best champagne, the finest brandy, and the most expensive cuts of meat, even when a hundred came to dinner. She was one of the first Washington hostesses to mix her guests, a trick she learned from the Algonquin Set in New York. She placed renowned reporters next to diplomats, actresses next to politicians, dowagers next to labor leaders. A typical guest list during the thirties might have included the Polish ambassador, a Cabinet officer, J. Edgar Hoover, labor leader Andy Furnuseth, Senator Burton K. Wheeler, Major General Patrick Hurley, Alger Hiss, Harold L. Ickes, John L. Lewis, Gene Tunney, Sumner Welles, Douglas Mac-

Arthur, Hearst, Brisbane, or Cissy's brother Joe. Sprinkled among the lions would be some of the best-looking girls in Washington, many of whom worked for Cissy's newspaper. Cissy provided glamour and entertainment and not just another place for diplomats and politicians to do business. There were song recitals, dances in the ballroom, and movies. Lovers and enemies were made at her parties, something rare for Washington.

"Cissy's circle," *Town & Country* magazine noted in April, 1935, "is the most explosive in the nation's capital. Cissy attracts people who are news, people who make news and people behind the news. There is even a hearing for those ahead of the news, the prophets without honor in their own districts."

Cissy stayed in or near the focus of her parties, regardless how large the gathering. She cut a striking figure in hostess pajamas or other clothes more daring than the normal styles of the day. Charles James, a leading couturier of the thirties, designed for her the kind of outfits ordinarily worn on the stage, and she used them as backdrops for her jewels. The magnificence of her black pearl necklace was matched only by her diamonds, one of the largest sets ever assembled by Cartier. Cissy's chic lay in the casual manner she wore her costumes, as if she had slipped into the first thing grabbed from the closet. She was always giving away her clothes. Once she saw a *Washington Star* reporter, Evelyn Peyton Gordon, shivering outside the Russian Embassy waiting for a story and impulsively lent her a sable coat. The next morning, when Miss Gordon returned the coat, Cissy said she might as well have kept it if she needed it.

Cissy had wonderful instincts as a hostess. At large

parties she kept her sharp tongue in check and refrained from drinking. She moved easily from one group to another, flattering the men, asking the women about their children and complimenting their clothes. But Cissy considered the big galas "an effort." Throughout the thirties she continued to entertain on the grand scale, but she turned over the details of arrangements and invitations to social secretaries and friends. Sometimes she didn't even bother to come to her own parties. More often than not Cissy ate by herself and then stayed up late, drinking and smoking and reading. Like her mother, she had become an insomniac. Occasionally she would creep down to the caverns of her kitchen and sit barefoot on the table, drinking beer with the night watchman. Then she and her poodles would go to bed—sometimes to the fourth floor, where she had lived as a debutante, and sometimes to her mother's second-floor room, with the balcony overlooking Dupont Circle.

Cissy's new career kept her so much in the city of Washington that she began looking for a place in the country where she could escape on bad days and weekends. She always felt better in the country. First she bought a large tract of land outside Potomac, Maryland, with a bluff overlooking the river. Then she discovered another piece of land, near Marlboro, Maryland, which included the remains of a seventeenth-century brick mansion that had recently burned down. Known as the Dower House because it had been a wedding present to a Custis and Lord Baltimore, the mansion was originally designed by young Christopher Wren as a hunting lodge for the Lords Baltimore, and later had served as an elegant country inn. The Dower House boasted a famous ghost, approved by the London Society for Psychical Research. The grounds were laid out by Major Pierre Charles L'Enfant, who developed the first city plan for Washington. The boxwood hedge in front of the house was from Mount Vernon and the tall stately trees ringing the terraced lawn were left over from the grounds of the United States Capitol, twenty-five miles away. Cissy unearthed the original plans for the mansion and commissioned an architect to restore the house around the huge chimneys left standing after the fire. The rooms were warm and rustic, with elegant woodwork and beamed ceilings.

At first Cissy instructed a storage company to ship a truckload of her furniture from New York to Maryland (she had twenty-five sideboards in a warehouse). But while the truck was on the road, Cissy decided against "decorating" Dower House. She sent the shipment of antiques back to storage, preferring to furnish her hideaway "simply," piece by piece as she went along. She added a swimming pool, stables, guest houses, and greenhouses to provide year-round flowers. She entertained there, but usually for "old-shoe" friends—Cal Carrington, Arthur Krock, Adela St. John, Lady Marjorie Broderick, and others.

Cissy went to Dower House as early as possible each spring and left when the hot sticky Maryland summer arrived. Then she transported the household to her Sands Point estate, Harbor Acres, where the cool Long Island breezes took the edge off the heat. In later years she added Miami, Southhampton, Palm Beach, Sarasota, and Nassau to her seasonal travel cycle. At such times she kept the whip cracking on the *Herald* by telegram and long-distance telephone calls. Editions of the paper were shipped wherever she went and she always had enough comments to run up huge telephone bills.

When Cissy signed a contract with Hearst, she assumed she had nothing to lose and everything to gain, as her aimless life had been growing sour. Actually, for an opinionated, outspoken woman, she was taking the biggest risk of her life. By hiring herself out as a celebrity editor, she renounced the immunity of her class and exposed herself to public censure as well as admiration. From the very beginning of her newspaper career, when she wrote a signed editorial denouncing a rival, she sat in a glass house pelting pebbles. A lonely and insecure woman, she had no protection against the day when her attacks would boomerang. She never anticipated the results of her actions. In fact, in a childish way, she expected approval.

It was one of Cissy's most charming characteristics that she always counted on a second chance. After a decade of fighting with Alice Roosevelt Longworth, Cissy confessed that she had a "leprous personality" and smilingly asked that all be forgiven. Mrs. Longworth's speechless refusal provoked a torrent of longshoreman's language such as the Somerset Club had never heard within its doors before; Cissy could not fathom Mrs. Longworth's reasons for bearing a grudge.* Remarkably, people did forgive Cissy most of the time—friends accepted apologies for grotesque insults; fired employees rejoined her payroll; spurned lovers scurried back. Those whom she stung with her newspaper did not forgive, however. Instead of a wasp she had become a one-woman hive.

* Cissy's fight with Mrs. Longworth inspired the Broadway play *First Lady.*

7

Sob Sister

It had been Cissy's experience that charm covered a multitude of sins. She expected her charm would work for the *Herald* if she could translate her personality into print. Brisbane and Hearst encouraged her to write for the paper in her own unorthodox style, bringing the readers to the doorstep of Cissy Patterson's world, its bright chandeliers and famous people. Never should the writings of a rich, red-headed celebrity editor be underplayed on account of triviality, Brisbane cautioned.

Most editors might consider trivial the observation that "men accuse women of talking too much because men want to talk a hundred per cent of the time." Cissy Patterson's two hundred and fifty word chat on the subject appeared in the *Herald's* editorial column. Her little editorial, "Talk," contained twenty sentences, five of them incomplete, and only one thought—that men talk more than women do. Most of it was devoted to two anecdotes, one about herself and the other about an "old colored Mammy." Her conclusion was that women babble but men "converse like sewing machines." Arthur Brisbane personally edited the "Talk" editorial. "You're a great editor, not Will Rogers," he reminded her. "Dignity, more dignity, *toujours* dignity."

"Once I get a bit more confidence, I won't bore you so much," Cissy started to reply, then caught herself before sending the letter. Brisbane, she knew, never accused her of being a boring writer, but a careless one. Much as she protested that she worked hard at writing ("I really sweat") Cissy's drafts tell a different story. Her method of writing was to seize upon an idea and transcribe it, either into a Dictaphone or onto a handy scrap of paper. She would rework it, crossing out words, making insertions, and scrawling sentences in the margins, but she would not rewrite if it did not work. She rarely wrote more than three hundred words. "I never was taught a thing about grammar," she insisted to Brisbane, "but I think I have a pretty good ear."

Brisbane suggested that concentration might improve that natural ear of hers. "It is wise not to use slang at all unless in quotation marks," he lectured. When strung together, her slang verbs, "slop," "gush" and "gabble," beat stridently against one another. "But there is something more terrible than [slang]," Brisbane continued "and that is your double negatives. I dare to say this, your younger admirers would not: we say in the English language 'not . . . or'. We don't say 'not . . . nor,' for that makes a double negative. Emphatically, you *should* write," he insisted when she threatened quitting. "My only suggestion is that you not put lugs on this type of writing. Make it bare and direct, less conversational and Cissy-esque."

Brisbane's carping irritated Cissy. In moments of pique she referred to him as a pompous, condescending old bore. She complained to Mr. Hearst that everyone except Brisbane complimented her writing. Just the same, Cissy kept submitting her material to Brisbane. She was smart enough to take free advice from a man at the top of his profession. At the salary Hearst paid him, Brisbane's time was worth at least $750 a day. Cissy's brother said that Arthur Brisbane was the greatest newspaperman of his time. Partly motivated by sincere affection, Cissy flattered the happily married septuagenarian with birthday presents, declarations of love, parties for his children at Dupont Circle, and bottles of choice wine. They carried on a delightfully flirtatious correspondence, warm and worldly and full of learned quotes. Mr. Brisbane, whom critics have called miserly and bitter, was a master of the amorous business letter. He drew silly little pictures of Cissy, dressed in Schiaparelli finery, batting her eyelashes and dropping her handkerchief. He used arrows to suggest the movement of her eyelashes.

In her early years running the *Herald,* Brisbane even wrote some of Cissy's by-line articles. Once, when Brisbane decided her subscribers would be interested in Cissy's views on an election contest, he dictated an editorial into a phonograph in the back seat of his limousine and sent it on from New York, and she ran it under her signature with minor style changes.

Cissy was as green as her cub reporters, but she had compensating assets, including her family name. That name opened the almost impenetrable door of the Florida villa in which "Scarface" Al Capone was holed up in 1931. Capone, surrounded by bodyguards, was not at home to reporters, but he received Cissy because she was Joe Patterson's sister. Capone had considered himself a friend of the whole family since the days of the gangster-ridden circulation wars in Chicago. Cissy wrote her exclusive interview with Capone in the manner of a society reporter recounting a visit to Buckingham Palace. She told how Capone's musclemen escorted her politely through the villa's wrought-iron gates into the great gangster's presence, how graciously he offered her a drink, and with a poignant note she mentioned his Christmas tree. He was, she reported, lonesome for Chicago, from which he had been "hounded out."

"My family, wife, my kid, my racket—they're all in Chicago," he told his guest. Cissy noted that the celebrated gray eyes narrowed to slits while he was explaining how "big business" persecuted him. "I done a favor for one of the big newspapers in the country when they was up against it," he reminded her. "Broke a strike for 'em. What do I get for doing 'em a favor?" Clucking sympathetically, Cissy admired Capone's powerful neck —strong enough to hold the weight of ten men, she ventured. "None of them big business guys can ever say I took a dollar from 'em," grumbled Scarface. "I only want to do business, you understand, with my own class. I don't interfere with their racket, they should let my racket alone." Cissy Patterson concluded: "It has been said many times that women have sympathy for gangsters. If you don't know why, consult Dr. Freud."

Cissy addressed herself *directly* to her readers. She used a woman-to-woman tone because, as she correctly reasoned, most of her readers were female. Women, she said, also buy newspapers, a fact she thought male editors too often overlooked. As an editor, however, Cissy tried not to commit the reverse sin of putting out an entire newspaper geared to female tastes. It was only in the special women's section and in her own writings that Cissy exclusively courted the ladies. And men, Cissy maintained, enjoyed eavesdropping on boudoir—not domestic—conversations.

Cissy's instinct for an untapped market was a family trait. In New York her brother Joe was winning an unparalleled circulation by aiming the *Daily News* at the common man. "Tell it to Sweeney," the newspaper's motto read, "the Stuyvesants will understand." In Washington, Cissy was telling it to Mrs. Sweeney. What would Mrs. Sweeney want to know about Al Capone? Why, that he was sexy, of course. It was as if Cissy, whenever she met a remarkable person or attended a glamorous function, sat down and wrote a letter to Mrs. Sweeney. "Well, what's she like?" the imaginary Mrs. Sweeney demanded to know about Eleanor Roosevelt in 1932. "This lady has solved the problem of living better than any woman I know," Cissy reported. "None of this business of self-destruction going on. . . . She never thinks about herself." Mrs. Sweeney was glad to know such a wonderful woman was in the White House, taking care of the President, during those hard times.

"Well, what did she say?" Mrs. Sweeney wanted to know when the assassinated Huey Long's widow came to Washington to fill out his term in the Senate in 1936. She said, "I'll do the best I can," according to Cissy's "Word Picture of a Fearless, Devoted Woman."

Homely details interested Mrs. Sweeney more than thoughtful analyses. She had heard of Dr. Albert Ein-

stein, of course, and knew him as the discoverer of a revolutionary scientific theory about "relativity." When Einstein came to America in 1931, Mrs. Sweeney saw his
sensitive face in the papers and followed his travels
around the country. Every woman wondered what *really*
went on in such a man's brain, not his theories but his
reactions to simple things. Cissy sat near Dr. Einstein at
the Hollywood premiere of Charlie Chaplin's *City Lights*.
She watched him during the performance and saw tears
flow from his eyes into the crinkles of his face. The *Herald*
ran it as a front-page story. Reader response was so enthusiastic that Cissy set out to get a personal interview
with Einstein. Her chance came while she was vacation-
ing in Palm Springs, California, at the same time the great
physicist was there as a houseguest of the tycoon, Samuel
Untermeyer. She knew Untermeyer, but Cissy did not
phone for an interview, guessing that Einstein wanted a
rest from the press. Instead she appeared in person at
Untermeyer's estate, where his servants informed her
Professor Einstein was walking in the desert. Servants
rarely questioned Cissy's purposes.

Cissy's front-page interview with Albert Einstein did
not contain a single quote. In fact, she never talked to
him. She had found Einstein on the desert, all right, but
he was stark naked, stretched out on the sand, sunbath-
ing. Arthur Brisbane chastised her for allowing modesty
to interfere with work. A great "sob sister" reporter like
Nellie Bly, he said, would have found a blanket, put it
over Dr. Einstein, and *got* the interview, if necessary sitting on the blanket to keep the subject at hand. Hearst,
on the other hand, complimented Cissy's little Einstein
non-interview. "We think it is your duty to come back to

San Simeon and interview us," he wired. "We made you what you are today, a great editor." Now Mrs. Sweeney knew Einstein sunbathed naked. And she knew Cissy Patterson had seen the genius without his clothes.

Cissy also dealt with the miseries of the Depression, a subject on which she might easily have offended Mrs. Sweeney, who was living in poverty or too close to it while Cissy was ensconced at Fifteen Dupont Circle, her fortune unimpaired. *The New York Daily News,* one source of her wealth, enjoyed its greatest growth period in the thirties. But Cissy's prose, flip, arrogant and gushing on other subjects, was compassionate and angry on the plight of the poor. And she demonstrated an understanding of the nature and dimension of the Depression in a manner pathetically lacking in some of her socially isolated high-society friends. Evalyn Walsh McLean, a warm-hearted and friendly leader of Washington's rich, responded to the searing sights of the Depression by wandering through the capital's streets indiscriminantly handing out five-dollar bills.

Joe Patterson had convinced Cissy that Mrs. Sweeney needed more than a five-dollar bill to tide her over. Joe Patterson's *Daily News* predicted the serious implications of the Depression while other newspapers were calling it a temporary panic, and he attributed his foresight to his eyesight. His fellow publishers, he said, would have known what was going on, if like him they walked the streets of New York every day, stood in the bread lines, and listened to the women talking on their doorsteps and the men talking in the bars. To say that the Depression would cure itself was as foolish as standing in a bread line and asking for toast.

"Joe is Joe and I am me," Cissy used to say. And as "me" she invariably veered off at her own angle, while following Joe's general direction. For "Cissy Goes to the Depression" she decided to dress like a maid and look for a job and write it up as a series for the paper.

The *Herald* followed every step of Cissy's descent into poverty, dramatizing with photographs how the odyssey began one night after an embassy ball. Like the Scarlet Pimpernel changing his identity to go on missions of mercy, Cissy stepped from an evening gown into a borrowed maid's "day-off" dress. Forsaking her apricot silk sheets, evoked in detail for *Herald* readers, Cissy disappeared into the December night to reappear as Maude Martin seeking Salvation Army charity. She had no money and no place to sleep, and though she had expected the experience to be exciting, she wrote that it was "dreary and depressing." Most disheartening was the night Cissy spent as Maude Martin at the Salvation Army headquarters in a room with four other women, tossing on a cot, listening to them cough and snore. Fifteen years later she remembered the Salvation Army matron in her will. With the aid of Washington's Life Adjustment Center, "Maude Martin" did find a job as a maid at five dollars a week. It was ironic testimony to the plight of the poor, Cissy observed, as she recalled how the matron told her she would go far with her looks and air of distinction. Even in shabby clothes Cissy did not look destitute. The aura of the very rich takes at least several weeks to wear off.

Cissy was progressive in her early newspaper days. With her brother and Hearst, she believed the government ought to spend money to relieve suffering. "Please," she wrote after a visit to the Emergency Relief Bureau, "private donations cannot take care of the destitute families in Washington. We are wholly dependent on the relief agencies." Her "Suffer Little Children" series in December, 1932, began a year-long campaign which resulted in Congress approving a hot-lunch program for D.C. schoolchildren. Cissy attacked the complexities of a government subsidy program with the same pungency that she carried on public feuds with Alice Longworth. At one point in the hot-lunch battle Cissy lectured a recalcitrant government official: "For four months, because of pedagogy, prejudice and red tape, nothing has been done. On February 2nd you were finally forced into a little talk about crackers and milk. Four months. A long wait for hungry children." Meantime, Cissy anonymously spent her own money on the project.

But Cissy was a greater animalarian than humanitarian. Her beloved poodles had the run of the office, and *Herald* staff men were expected to take due note of them with an occasional pat. In her newspaper Cissy conducted an endless campaign against vivisection. She shared with Hearst and Marion Davies a horror of medical experiments on animals and she ran gruesome pictures and outraged stories of dogs and cats undergoing operations or other trials at medical schools.

One winter Cissy heard that the ducks in Washington's Rock Creek Park were unable to break through the ice for food and were starving. With appropriate promotion in the *Herald*, Cissy hired a helicopter to drop bundles of food to the hungry birds. The packages, unfortunately, landed on the closely gathered ducks, killing a number of them.

[*111*]

Cissy mounted another rescue operation when the Washington Zoo's gorilla, N'Gni, contracted pneumonia. She arranged for an oxygen tent to be flown by air express from New York to Washington. But the *Herald*'s chronicle of the mercy mission was cut short when N'Gni died— in Cissy's tent.

Cissy had a talent for starting little brush fires in odd corners. She recommended laxer divorce laws, legalized gambling, and a national lottery to help pay off the National Debt. At the suggestion of her friend Ethel Barrymore she campaigned for abolition of D.C. restrictions against the use of child actors. When she learned that her newsprint shipments would cost less by water, she told her city desk to generate some enthusiasm for barge traffic on the Potomac. And when she was told by the FBI that it was too understaffed to help solve the murder of a *Herald* carrier man, she launched a drive to allocate more men and money to the Justice Department, a theme which all Hearst newspapers picked up.

The most useful compaigns Cissy launched at the *Herald* concentrated on local problems. She had told Hearst from the beginning that the *Herald* would be brighter and more useful with less of his canned features and more local initiative. She proved it, advocating in the *Herald* an array of reforms for the District of Columbia. Most notable in view of later charges that she was a racist, Cissy backed suffrage for the voteless citizens of Washington, despite the prognosis that suffrage would give the majority of political power to Negroes.

In 1932 Cissy went to the Democratic Convention in Chicago as one of Hearst's privileged executives, and had a bird's-eye view of the political infighting that engaged much of W.R.'s energies. But Cissy, cribbing over Brisbane's shoulder, wrote mostly color pieces for the *Herald*. She described the "swell" crowds, the security precautions, and wondered out loud why Heywood Brown wore "a hat like a potato chip." She saw in the audience the celebrated prizefighter Gene Tunney, and noted for her readers that he was "perspiring like a little child" in the heat of the Stockyards Amphitheater. The convention was a particularly exciting one with a number of memorable and unexpected sidelights. In one instance Cissy's new friend Huey Long gave a vivid example of his political finesse, when he captured the podium microphone and begged the hissing convention audience: "Don't applaud me, don't applaud me!" The Kingfish knew he was being hissed but Louisiana voters listening to the radio didn't.

Cissy's impression of her first Democratic Convention was of stifling heat, endless talk, and Byzantine maneuvering. With exasperation she wrote that Roosevelt was nominated by a political convention "based on methods of the third degree." She was impatient, Cissy confided to *Herald* readers, to be off to her Long Island estate, where the cool breezes of the Sound and her poodles awaited her.

On the other hand, Inauguration day, March 5, 1933, was a raw day. Sitting on a folding chair, waiting for the arrival of the outgoing and incoming Presidents, Cissy wrote that she grew numb in her sable coat. She mentioned the names of her famous friends present, what they wore, and paid homage to Roosevelt's infectious good humor. But the thrust of her article, laced through all the pleasantries, was Cissy's concern for the tragic figure of Hoover. Recoiling at the sight of the dishonored leader, she observed, "I have seen people once or twice standing at the brink of an open grave with the same kind of despair."

In the course of her natural if rapid evolution as a newspaperwoman Cissy gradually lost enthusiasm for covering breaking events and writing shallow, talky profiles of celebrities. Such reporting, she discovered, became repetitious. She had wanted to imprint her personality on the *Herald* and she had succeeded. Now the trick was to keep her audience intrigued by that personality, to expose a garter but not too much leg. Cissy never gave up writing for the *Herald,* but she tried to enhance her by-line by reserving it for reasonably substantial interviews and for statements of policy, whimsical, vicious, or otherwise.

In a 1937 interview with her close friend John L. Lewis, president of the United Mine Workers Union, Cissy attempted to add weight to her newspaper reporting. She still included the feminine angle—how she happened to have lunch with Lewis, where and what they ate and how he looked. But she also found room for his comments on the New Deal. "There is too much time given to balancing political personalities," Lewis barked, "and not enough given to applying the seat of the pants to the seat of the chair." Lewis concluded that the second-term New Deal, which he had supported strongly, was foundering.

Cissy's development as a reporter disappointed Arthur Brisbane. Initially he expected that her shrewd intelligence would compensate for her educational deficiencies. He knew that she was incapable of organizing material, and that while her intuitive powers were sharp, her logic

Joseph Medill,
patriarch of the Chicago Tribune.

Cissy's mother, Elinor Medill Patterson, a great
beauty, in a portrait by Anders Zorn.

Papa, Robert Wilson Patterson, Jr.,
editor of the Chicago Tribune.

The four young cousins with their grandfather-patriarch Joseph Medill. From left to right: Bertie (Col. Robert Rutherford McCormick, the Chicago Tribune); Cissy (Eleanor Medill Patterson, Washington Times-Herald); Joseph Medill; J. Medill Mc-Cormick (U.S. Senator); and Capt. Joseph Medill Patterson (New York Daily News).

Cissy and her brother, Captain Joe, whom she adored, in a benign moment. (JACKIE MARTIN)

Cissy in the composing room of the Times-Herald *with Chief Compositor Irving Belt and Society Editor Ruth Jones.* (JACKIE MARTIN)

Col. Robert Rutherford McCormick, Cissy's first cousin.

Cissy and William Randolph Hearst, her journalistic sponsor, reading the much disputed comics. The right of Hearst to publish these was eventually brought into court. (JACKIE MARTIN)

1943, Cissy and Alice Roosevelt Longworth "make up" at the Dower House after many misunderstandings and a long public row.

Portrait of the Artist

E.P

Cissy's conception of herself.
(JACKIE MARTIN)

was not; but he thought that if she learned to ask good questions, she would elicit good answers. After working with Cissy for a while, Brisbane concluded she would not fulfill her promise as a newspaper writer. She was too distracted.

Cissy's inability to capitalize fully on the rare reporting opportunities open to her had never been more apparent than in the summer of 1934 when she traveled to Europe with Hearst. Wherever the Chief traveled, he took along a large party of newspaper and movie friends to entertain him between audiences with heads of state, treating his guests to background briefings as well as antiques. His 1934 itinerary included Spain, Great Britain (not France, he was scrapping with France), Italy (Mussolini wanted to talk to him), Belgium, Holland, and Germany (where he said he would like to see Hitler). With W.R. as guide and with her languages and European contacts, Cissy might have collected material for an important series. Political developments abroad had moved rapidly since Mussolini's proposal for a four-power pact to contain the Nazi menace had failed in March, 1933. Russia had attempted to form a solid bloc from the Baltic to the Middle East; France, in the wake of its worst internal crisis since 1919, was moving toward the East European powers; and Nazi Germany was on the verge of announcing her withdrawal from the Disarmament Conference and the League of Nations, indirectly breaking with the West.

Cissy initially declined Hearst's invitation, even though his mistress, Marion Davies, had confidently booked space for her on the ocean liner *Rex*. A Hearst telegram was immediately forthcoming: SINCE YOU DO NOT COME ABROAD WHEN I ASK YOU STOP PRETTY SOON I AM GOING

TO GET VERY UPPITY AND NOT DO ANYTHING YOU TELL ME
STOP. Brisbane persuaded Cissy to go at least to New
York and "give W.R. one last farewell look from under
that broadbrimmed hat before he sails." Not until Hearst
and Miss Davies' "fun group" were in Spain did Cissy
change her mind. In July she was persuaded by Hearst's
magazine executive, Richard Berlin, and his general manager, Thomas J. White, to sail with them to England and
join the Chief there. Her romantic feelings for White undoubtedly influenced her decision. She had fallen in love
with him, though she said two people "with the combined
ages of two hundred and fifty ought to have better sense."
The genial pug-nosed Tom White was married, Roman
Catholic, and the father of five children.

Aboard their ship, by an odd coincidence, was one of
Hearst's art dealers, Ernst Hanfstaengel, who operated a
shop in New York. "Putzi," as friends called him, served
the Third Reich as a propaganda expert and was known
as one of Hitler's intimate advisors. Cissy tagged him
"The Brain Behind Hitler." Hanfstaengel granted Cissy
an interview—any friend of his good customer, William
Randolph Hearst, was a friend of Hanfstaengel's. He refused, however, any discussion of politics, insisting on talk
of love and music with a pretty lady. Cissy squeezed a
Herald front-page story from the interview, but she had
to "write off the wall."

After farewells with the oily Dr. Hanfstaengel, Cissy,
White, and Berlin embarked with the Hearst party to
Glamorganshire on the Bristol Channel in Wales, where
the Chief owned one of the finest Norman buildings in
Great Britain—St. Donant's Castle. But Cissy quarreled
with Tom White, and fled to Paris before Hearst even had

a chance to show her his newly installed Elizabethan great chamber. "Tom has described to me your sudden vanishing from the party," Brisbane wrote Cissy. "There is nothing remarkable in that. Compared to you, Puck in the *Midsummer Night's Dream* was an old-fashioned one-cylinder Cadillac."

In Paris Cissy went to the couture openings with Tom White's sister, Carmel Snow, editor of *Vogue,* and she cabled home stories on the Vionet and Schiaparelli shows which, she said, were "so far as I know the first fashion stories cabled out of Paris." Then she went home after scarcely a month in Europe, using as an excuse "my great age." As Cissy was leaving Paris, Mrs. Carmel Snow told her, "You will surely fall in love with my brother. Everyone falls in love with my brother Tom." During two solitary days at sea Cissy pondered the proposition, and then she radioed Mrs. Snow: WELL YOU SHOULD MEET MY BROTHER JOE.

Had she stayed with the Hearst party, Cissy might have met Hitler. "Putzi" Hanfstaengel appeared in Munich, freely offering his services to Mr. Hearst as a guide and art advisor. He "fastened himself to the party," according to William Randolph Hearst, Jr. While dispensing cultural lessons to the Americans, Hanfstaengel dispatched releases to the German press about Mr. Hearst's enthusiasm for the Reich, including a fictitious Hearst quote about Hitler's value to humanity. Finally, at Putzi's urging, Hitler summoned Hearst for a private interview. Cissy missed a big story in Germany, but it was a lucky miss. Hearst's visit with the Führer, even though it was a newspaper interview, created an uproar among American liberals and convinced many people that he was an out-

and-out fascist. If she had been there, Cissy's own un-
sophisticated view of Hitler might well have gotten her in
worse trouble than Hearst.

Cissy often needed protection from her judgment, "I
get what the psychiatrists call 'compulsions,'" she once
said, understating the case. Brisbane attempted to be
Cissy's guardian from the time he helped Hearst recruit
her. Again and again he persuaded Cissy not to continue
wild and foolish journalistic schemes. Her secretaries understood Brisbane's role, and they called on him in emer-
gencies. Such an emergency occurred in 1933, when
Cissy's ex-son-in-law, Drew Pearson, published *More
Merry-Go-Round,* an "inside" book containing gossip
about Cissy and her friends which Pearson had learned
by having the run of Dupont Circle. Pearson, who collaborated with reporter Robert Allen on the venture, had
lost his job at the *Baltimore Sun* a year earlier with publication of the book's predecessor, *The Washington Merry-
Go-Round.*

Brisbane obtained a reviewer's copy and, anticipating
Cissy's reaction, telephoned from New York to her secretary, Carolyn Shaw. He and Mrs. Shaw agreed that Brisbane must see Cissy before Cissy saw the book. Cissy was
then isolated in her railroad car, returning from the West
Coast, and was not due to reach Washington for several
hours. Brisbane still had time to travel from New York to
Washington. But Mrs. Shaw and Brisbane were unaware
that Cissy had stopped in Chicago to buy a copy of *More
Merry-Go-Round.* Ahead of her scheduled arrival, she
rushed into Fifteen Dupont Circle, "mad as a snake" and
shouting for "Callie" (Mrs. Shaw) to take dictation.
What could a secretary do? While Cissy paced up and
down the office, reciting a four-letter-word litany, Mrs.

Shaw changed her typewriter ribbon, tore three different pages, erased words, and spilled ink. Cissy fired her and rehired her twice during the sitting. At last, when Cissy had nearly finished dictating a cannibalistic anti-Pearson editorial, Brisbane arrived. He was an old man and quite ill, but he verbally wrestled Cissy to the ground.

Brisbane was, however, less and less able to put out the time and energy needed to harness Cissy. In his place came other newspaper figures, including a young Tennessean, Frank Waldrop, who endured Cissy's quixotic nature to become her executive editor and one of her closest advisors.

Waldrop's first big assignment for Cissy was to write, for use under her by-line, a description of poverty in Appalachia. The idea for the series, billed "Dixie's Dead End," came to Cissy while she was motoring north from Florida through the destitute Secquatchia Valley. She gave Waldrop precise instructions:

ONE GO TO RUGBY THIRTY MILES FROM HARRIMAN TENNESSEE AND GET PHOTOGRAPHS OF MRS BERTRAM WITH HER EIGHT CHILDREN STOP DONT LET THEM WASH OR DRESS UP STOP.

Into the "Dixie's Dead End" series, as into all the writing on her newspaper which particularly interested her, Cissy inserted her pet phrases and opinions. She instructed Waldrop to emphasize that Appalachian *women* "labored all their lives as bonded slaves while their men loafed and laughed."

"Dixie's Dead End" was the most popular series the *Herald* ever ran under Cissy's by-line. There was an extra savor to that success because, as Cissy noted, she "found" Appalachian poverty before Roosevelt did.

8

A Pound of Flesh

Cissy wanted the *Washington Herald* to be first in advertising, first in street sales, and first in home delivery. She had told her brother she could make a success in the newspaper business and she meant to do it, no matter what it cost in money or friends. She considered her sex and education such formidable handicaps that she did not feel obliged to be ethical as well. Men could afford ethics. Cissy never pretended to be a gentleman. Cissy was therefore sorry when a friend and a gentleman bought the *Washington Post,* her competition. She had known Eugene Meyer since he came to Washington in 1917 as an advisor to the War Industries Board. "Governor" Meyer enjoyed respect even from political enemies. He had made a fortune on Wall Street and had served as chairman of Hoover's Federal Reserve Board.

Cissy and Meyer's wife, Agnes, became friends at a White House lunch in 1917, and Cissy dined often at the palatial Meyer residence on Crescent Place. Agnes and Cissy chatted at length on the telephone and regularly rode together in Rock Creek Park, a sunken green strip running through the heart of residential Washington.

The Meyers, as Cissy suspected, were among her competitors seeking to acquire the *Washington Post* from the McLean family after Edward McLean's financial and emotional breakdown in 1929. Cissy lightly warned Eugene Meyer that she would not forgive him if he snatched the *Post* away from her, and she maintained that he had promised not to. But Meyer changed his mind after his retirement from the Federal Reserve Board. "One day," his wife recalls, "he came downstairs, ran his finger along the bannister, and said the house was not right. So I said, 'Eugene, it's time you bought the *Washington Post.*' "

The Post Company assets were auctioned off in June, 1931, on the steps of its old building on Pennsylvania Avenue, two blocks south of the White House. Cissy attended, wearing a fashionable slouch hat and a grim expression. Tom White, her good friend and the general manager of the Hearst newspapers, and *Herald* business manager William C. Shelton, came along to advise her. Cissy wanted to buy the *Post,* but she was torn between conflicting pieces of advice. Brother Joe warned her that she would "lose her shirt." Arthur Brisbane, who had once owned the Washington *Times* and then sold it to Hearst, promised that it was better to spend Hearst's money than one's own. Cissy invited Hearst into the *Post* venture, but he would agree only to buy the newspaper's controlling stock instead of its assets, an offer which the McLean family declined.

Many parties were interested in the property, among them the Gannett Chain of newspapers and a group of investors backing newsman David Lawrence. One rumored prospective buyer was Alice Roosevelt Longworth. The bidding went higher than expected. When two lawyers representing the anonymous Eugene Meyer bid a $850,000, Cissy's advisors were of two minds and the result was inaction. Thomas White scowled negatively and proved to be the restraining influence. Later William Shelton told Cissy she should have gone another million dollars if necessary. "I just bet it's Eugene Meyer!" Cissy exclaimed, angry and discouraged. She immediately called Agnes Meyer in Mount Kisco, but the Meyers had decided to remain anonymous while the property was in receivership.

Only in June of 1933 did Eugene Meyer reveal his identity. "Since we could not have the *Post* for ourselves," Arthur Brisbane consoled Cissy, "I am glad Eugene has got it, for he is an extremely fine young man with plenty of ambition and he will give you a run for your money, which is important for *your* ambition. . . . Mr. Hearst agrees with me thoroughly in regard to Mr. Meyer. He is a businessman, not a psychopath, who will be able to discuss propositions of benefit to both our papers. . . ."

Cissy was not so philosophical. The *Post,* though it had been asleep under McLean management, was a potentially better newspaper than the *Herald.* Cissy knew that Eugene Meyer would spend the money to make it the best morning paper in Washington. Though Cissy was bragging in April, 1933, that the *Herald*'s advertising had increased 251,000 lines over the previous year and that its circulation had broken a record for Washington morning newspapers, she kept an eye over her shoulder, knowing Meyer would bring his new product up. She started pirating the *Post*'s assets even before she was sure Eugene Meyer owned it. She spent as much money as Hearst would give her to hire away *Post* employees. During those lean Depression years, she discovered, money would buy just about anybody.

However, incredibly, even Mr. Hearst was running out of money. In 1932 an emergency council of Hearst executives at San Simeon decided that the $63,000,000 drop in annual advertising revenues demanded a general salary cut just when Cissy was trying to attract people from the *Post*.

The *Post* assets included a contract with the Chicago Tribune Company for certain outstandingly popular features, including the comic strips "Andy Gump," "Winnie Winkle," "Gasoline Alley," "Skeezix," "Dick Tracy," and "Little Orphan Annie." In this period of American journalism, comic strips attracted a bigger readership than any other section of a newspaper, including hard news. The *New York News-Chicago Tribune* comics enjoyed a star following, the largest in the business. The *News-Tribune* cartoons had been contracted to the *Washington Post* on a five-year basis long before Cissy edited the *Washington Herald*. She, as a major *Tribune-News* stockholder, was a party to the contract, which included a renewal option to go into effect at its expiration date in the spring of 1933. The *Tribune-News* feature salesmen understood the clear intention of the Washington Post Company under whatever ownership, to retain the features which sold thousands of *Post*s every day.

Cissy wanted the comic strips. Her brother Joe, after all, was fairy godfather to the cartoon characters. He had christened Sidney Smith's "Gump" family with old Mrs.

Patterson's favorite description for foolish behavior: their mother's warning that Joe and Cissy had grown up hearing: "Don't be such a gump!"

Patterson attributed his remarkable success as a publisher to his ability to communicate with the common man. Going on his usual assumption that what interested him would interest the average reader, Captain Joe had told cartoonist Frank King to draw a strip about motor cars. On his incessant walks through the streets and alleys of Chicago he had noticed how many people spent Sundays tinkering with cars. "Gasoline Alley," he told Frank King, would make a fine title for the strip. Later "Skeezix," named after a baby boy whom Frank King found abandoned on his doorstep, toddled into "Gasoline Alley," and "Skeezix" became the first cartoon character to grow up under a readership's eyes.

Cissy's brother, wooing the expanding New York working-girl population, helped create and chose the name for "Winnie Winkle the Breadwinner." He gave Frank Henry Willard his title for "Moon Mullins" from the PLUMBERS section of the classified telephone directory. Joe Patterson talked about cartoon characters as if they were his neighbors, and he loved meddling with their affairs. Usually his suggestions anticipated exactly what the readership wanted from Moon and Winnie and the others; usually the artists thanked him for interfering, although Patterson, too, could be wrong. He was very wrong about "Daddy Warbucks" when artist Harold Lincoln Gray introduced "Daddy" as Annie's best friend. "Who ever heard of a rich orphan?" Joe Patterson snorted. When he cut the strip out of the paper, he got his answer from hundreds of people who called the paper and threatened to cancel their subscriptions unless "Annie" came home to her pages the very next day. She did.

Cissy felt Joe's cartoon-strip characters were part of the family. Chester Gould's "Tracy" detective, named "Dick" by Joe, was a favorite offspring. So was Moon Mullins. Legal fine points aside, Cissy thought the *Washington Post* had no right to employ these Patterson children when she wanted to use them herself for Hearst's *Herald*.

Cissy anticipated that her brother and her cousin Bert might object if she interfered with the operation of the News-Tribune Syndicate on behalf of a Hearst newspaper. Captain Patterson and Colonel McCormick were not in business to help Citizen Hearst. But neither did they wish to cope with Cissy's temper, and so they gave her limp co-operation. Cissy was visiting Hearst at his San Simeon castle over Christmas, 1932, when she telephoned the News-Tribune Syndicate sales department. "This is Mrs. *Patterson*," she said, daring the salesman, William Crawford, to doubt it. Explaining that the contracts of the Washington Post Company had been invalidated by change of ownership, a transparent falsehood, she requested that the syndicate transfer all *News-Tribune* features from the *Post* to the *Washington Herald*, effective immediately.

Cissy succeeded in buying the coveted feature material for two months, but only because the Post Company was still in receivership and suffering from delayed reactions. In February, however, the News-Tribune Syndicate wrote up a new five-year contract with the Post Company and jerked the comics away. She had no right to be, but Cissy was mad. "I guess when I telephoned Crawford from San Simeon he came down [to Washington] and did some slick bargaining," she said. In a wire to Hearst she implied that if he cared enough about his *Herald,* he could get her comics back for her. It was expecting rather a lot. Monarch though he might be in his own organization, Mr. Hearst's authority did not extend to the operations of the *Washington Post* or the *Chicago Tribune* or the *New York Daily News.*

NEVER MIND THE TRIBUNE FEATURES, the Chief wired Cissy. I AM PERFECTLY SATISFIED NOT TO HAVE THEM AND DO NOT THINK THE POST WILL AMOUNT TO ANYTHING UNLESS THEY GET OUR EDITOR AND PUBLISHER. Cissy might have appreciated such flattery from the publisher himself. Not all Hearst editors who made demands upon the Chief received such prompt, courteous treatment. Most Hearst editors, fearing that further action on the matter might irritate Hearst and cost them their jobs, would have ceased. Cissy understood that Hearst meant her to drop the comics issue. In the margin of his telegram she penciled, "*Now* how do I act!" Cissy did act. "*This* is Mrs. Patterson," she reminded the News-Tribune Syndicate for the second time. When she was through talking, she had persuaded the syndicate to break its new contract with the *Post*—this time on the grounds that the *Post*'s new anonymous owner had *delayed* in assuring the *News-Tribune* of his intentions to continue his feature subscriptions. "Little Orphan Annie" came over to the *Herald* again.

In June of 1933, while Cissy was backing the *News-Tribune* salesman against the drawing-room wall in Dupont Circle, Eugene Meyer announced his identity as the *Post*'s publisher. Cissy sniffed that it was no news to her.

She was not surprised that within his first days as publisher, Mr. Meyer addressed himself to Cissy's sleight of hand with his comics. Cissy's mistake was in thinking that she could bamboozle him. In a friendly businesslike way Meyer asked the News-Tribune Company to stop playing games and to make good on its contract, since, as any intelligent person could see, there was no legal basis for breaking it which would stand up in a law court. Accustomed though he and his wife were to Cissy's shenanigans, business was business. When informed of Meyer's uncompromising attitude, Cissy called him at his summer home in New York. Apparently she thought that if he understood how *personally* she felt about the comics, her own family comics, he would relent. He was sorry to have to turn her down. "You know," she said in a low voice, "of course, Eugene, this means a fight." He said he knew.

"The matter is now in the hands of our lawyers," Meyer informed Mr. Hearst, his personal friend, in a letter dated June 26, 1933. "But I would rather deal with this in a friendly way." Hearst saw the makings of a good story: an epic battle between tycoons, both amateurs in the newspaper business, one a former chairman of the Federal Reserve Board, the other a glamorous woman. Much as he respected Meyer, Hearst could not bring himself to stop the fight, especially when he considered the publicity value. Washing his hands of any guilt which otherwise might wipe off on him, Mr. Hearst turned the situation over to Brisbane, who placed the blame on the Patterson-McCormick newspaper empire. Brisbane drafted a warm, engaging reply to Meyer, explaining, gentleman to gentleman, that while he and Hearst understood the *Post*'s position, and while they wanted to do everything they could to help, they dared not interfere with Cissy. "Mrs. Patterson, I am afraid, would not welcome my meddling," he confided.

Somehow Cissy was surprised that August to find herself involved in a lawsuit. WASNT I A SAP? she wired Hearst. Hearst knew better. Lawsuits took time; meanwhile Cissy, reluctantly supported by the Tribune Company, kept printing the comics. And meanwhile people kept buying the *Herald* for Cissy's reaction to the lawsuit. Cissy's reactions, unusual in sedate Washington, harked back to the rowdy journalism of Grandfather Medill who called opposition publisher Cyrus McCormick a patent thief and a Confederate sympathizer on the *Tribune* editorial pages. In the twentieth century the trend was toward milder journalistic tongue-lashings, but Cissy couldn't resist telling what she thought about Eugene Meyer and the *Washington Post*.

Among numerous slighting references to the *Post* the pages of the *Herald* (including a caricature drawing of the *Post*'s symbolic crowing cock), two instances went down as freaks in journalistic history.

The first was occasioned by the trial of Bruno Hauptmann for the kidnaping of Charles Lindbergh's infant son. Cissy's good friend, star reporter Adela Rogers St. John, covered the trial for the Hearst newspapers, and her assessment of the case against Hauptmann caused President Roosevelt to tell her that she had convinced him of Hauptmann's guilt. Cissy's *Herald* carried Miss St. John and all the other roving Hearst organization reporters assigned to the famous trial. Meyer's *Post*, not being a chain newspaper, relied upon its own reporters and the wire services. On Valentine's Day, 1935, at the high point of Cissy's fight with Meyer, the *Post* crossed signals and printed an edition with the headline: HAUPTMANN GUILTY BUT ESCAPES ELECTRIC CHAIR, when, in fact, Bruno Hauptmann had been sentenced to die. The *Post* had compounded its error by calling the story a scoop. Although the *Post* editors caught the error before the edition went out on the streets, one of Cissy's reporters obtained a copy from the *Post*'s office and fetched it home to the *Herald* to be photographed.

FALSE VERDICT FOOLS READERS—WRONG AGAIN! Under this weird headline Cissy's *Herald* printed a facsimile of the pertinent portion of the offending *Post*, presenting it as if the *Post* hadn't caught its drastic error.

When Meyer ignored the challenge, Cissy took drastic action. She wrote a signed editorial charging Eugene Meyer with frauding the Audit Bureau of Circulation. The *Washington Post*, that week, had been reproducing photographs of piles of their newspapers which they alleged had been stolen and dumped by teen-age vandals. In a public letter headed YOU ASKED FOR IT, EUGENE, Cissy called Meyer's *Post* a liar:

> Dear Eugene,
> I wonder if you know that the photographs reproduced Monday and Tuesday in full page announcements in the *Washington Post* were taken by *Washington Herald* photographers in the presence of a representative of the Audit Bureau of Circulation.
> Could you imagine that copies of these photos and similar ones have been locked in my desk since September 19, 1934?
> Do you know that the papers represented are all *Washington POSTS*? Would you be surprised, Eugene, to learn that none of these papers were ever put into

the racks nor were they ever distributed to the public?

Are you so innocent that you believe that papers stolen singly, as you infer, collect all by themselves into bundles of hundreds mostly bound up with twine?

Would you be terribly surprised to learn that none of those papers were ever stolen by the Washington public, in whom you have so little faith?

But, as a matter of fact, were they ever intended for the public? Has the thought never occurred to you that they were probably never out of the hands of your own employees?

You have so little faith in human nature, Eugene, that you may not believe me when I tell you that thousands of other copies of the *reliable Washington Post* were dumped at the same time in other localities. We have photos of those other ones also. Would you like to see them?

Were those thousands stolen by the Washington public, as you have said Eugene, or were they *dumped* papers which the *Washington Post* in its circulation figures claimed as not paid? I wonder if you have yet discovered that the Audit Bureau of Circulation will not permit you to call this paid circulation.

I'm not very old in the newspaper business, Eugene, but you are even younger than I. Possibly when you are a little more experienced you will learn to have as real a faith in the Washington public as I have always had.

Sincerely yours, Eleanor Patterson.

"People in glass houses shouldn't throw stones," was one of Cissy's favorite maxims. In fact she borrowed from it for the title of her first novel. In charging Meyer with dumping papers to pad his circulation, Cissy was indeed occupying a glass house, for the *Herald* was up to the same game.

Cissy feuded with zest. She enjoyed it, and she communicated her joy to her superiors within the Hearst organization. KEEP UP THE GOOD WORK, telegraphed W.R. after the publication of her open letter. I GUESS EUGENE KNOWS WHERE HE STANDS NOW. YOU SWING A WICKED PEN.

Arthur Brisbane gleefully conspired with Cissy against the *Post*. At her flirtatious prodding, he wrote a letter to Sears Roebuck's General Robert Wood, a well-known admirer of the *Chicago Tribune,* on the subject of advertising. General Wood, Brisbane suggested, would rather have a Patterson succeed in Washington journalism than a Meyer. "Mr. Eugene Meyer, who has bought the *Post,* is a good friend of mine," Mr. Brisbane wrote, "and I would not, if all things were even, suggest anything that might be harmful to him. But he is an enormously rich man, doesn't need the money, and I think you ought to switch Sears advertising to Mrs. Patterson." General Wood said he would investigate the matter at once. "Of course personally I would rather see advertising in the *Herald* than in the *Post,*" he agreed, "for while I respect and admire Eugene Meyer as a man, I think his monetary policy is 100% wrong."

There was an engaging quality about the *Herald's* promotion of "Gasoline Alley" and all the other cartoon characters who rightfully belonged to the *Post*. Cissy's newspaper staged parades with floats and showed "Dick Tracy" cartoons at neighborhood movie houses, daring Eugene Meyer to do something about it. Two years after Meyer asked for his comics, the Supreme Court ordered Cissy to return them. Stalling to the end, Cissy told the *Post* that the *Herald* had already made up its color-page features for the following Sunday. Eugene Meyer agreed to her publishing the Sunday comics on condition that she also print a front-page box, acknowledging her debt to the *Post*. Cissy thought Mr. Meyer's request ungallant, so when Sunday came, the *Herald* printed the features, but no front-page box.

When Meyer saw the boxless Sunday *Herald*, he took what Cissy considered petty action. He ordered his editors to insert into the Sunday *Post*'s second edition the agreement letting Mrs. Patterson use his features one more time on condition she admit to whom they belonged. Twisting the knife, the *Post* charged Cissy with flouting the agreement. Cissy was so angry when she read the *Post*'s second edition that she jerked the expensive color features out of the *Herald* and substituted others which the News-Tribune Syndicate rushed to Washington by air express. As she stared at the *Post*'s six-column editorial cartoon, depicting the Supreme Court as a robed figure sternly ordering Andy Gump and company toward the *Post* front page—"To your Post"—Cissy entertained murderous thoughts. She wanted to cause Eugene Meyer pain. Shakespeare came to her aid.

Inspired by *The Merchant of Venice*, Cissy asked the butler at Dupont Circle to get from the chef a pound of raw beefsteak. She told her secretary to order from Small's Florist a spray of freesia, a bunch of sweet peas, and some forget-me-nots. From the housekeeper she obtained a pretty box, and in it she put the pound of raw meat, covered with the flowers, and around the box she tied a ribbon: a gorgeous package. At last, she attached a card. "So as not to dissappoint you," she wrote. Then Cissy sent her chauffeur to deliver the poison to the

Meyer mansion on Crescent Place. Months later, after *Time* Magazine among other publications, had reported the "Shylock" prank to the nation, Cissy admitted that she had been rash. Her former friends, Eugene Meyer and his wife, Agnes, were deeply offended by the Shylock reference. "We were hurt," Mrs. Meyer recalls. "I guess I made a mistake that time," Cissy told an interviewer.

Cissy's former son-in-law, Drew Pearson, understanding that Cissy longed for a reconciliation with the Meyers, contrived that they meet. He convinced Mrs. Sumner Welles to invite them to the same dinner party. The Meyers arrived first, and the rest of the dinner guests fairly gasped when they saw Cissy walk in, because everybody in Washington knew that Eugene Meyer and Cissy did not speak to each other. Cissy rose to the occasion. She sailed over to Eugene, threw her arms around him, and said, "Let's be friends." According to Pearson, they laughed about their fight and ended up the evening by singing a little song together.

"But we really didn't see much of Cissy after that," Mrs. Meyer remembers.

9

The Hen House

Hearst's *Washington Herald* was a backwater newspaper office until Cissy arrived. Employees who were no longer useful to the Hearst organization were pensioned off there—the alcoholics, the weary old-timers, the malingerers. The atmosphere in the city room was stale and a little desperate, as in a Siberian garrison town. The troops performed—they were professionals—but without spirit. Cissy's arrival changed the air. "All I have to offer the *Herald* is dynamite," she said. "I'd rather raise hell than vegetables any day."

A former *Herald* copy boy remembers that every time she walked through the city room the "working stiffs" sat straighter in their chairs. She was a perpetual event. She might fire someone. She might give someone a raise. She might seek out the lowliest cub reporter and compliment him on a story. She might insult the city editor in front of everyone.

Before Cissy assumed editorship the *Washington Herald* had been a masculine haven. It smelled of cigar smoke and the language spoken there was as rich as manure. After every edition the desk men disappeared for a drink, and certain people in the office rarely sobered up. "It wasn't an intellectual paper," one picture editor affectionately recalls. When Cissy assumed editorship, the cigar smoke and the language and the drinking remained. The added ingredient was women. Cissy hired so many women that wags at the National Press Club, a bastion of masculinity, called the *Herald* "Cissy's Hen House." The men snickered, but they also stared. Never before had so many beautiful women worked for one newspaper. Charming girls, Cissy insisted, enjoyed advantages over other reporters—doors opened to them which men found closed. Not that Cissy expected her girl reporters to cover beats or important hard news; she used the seasoned Hearst staff for those assignments. "I cannot believe that women have caught up with men yet," she admitted in a radio speech. "But the best of them are smart enough to gold-dig on men's ideas."

Cissy recruited her girls from horse shows, dinner parties, kitchens, and offices. She demanded no previous journalistic training, just "sparkle" and "punch." Pretty finishing school graduates with rich fathers, she realized, were a particularly inexpensive source of labor. And one could fire them without worrying about their dependents. Admittedly, few of these knew how to write, but the absurdity of their prose carried its own particular appeal. One curvaceous member of the student staff ended an interview with Mr. District of Columbia, a beauty king, with the statement: "I swear, I would be *terrified* of all those muscles!"

Cissy's "hens" laid golden eggs for the feature department and for the women's pages, otherwise known as

"Cissy's playground." They covered Society in Society's language. They repeated little "tit-bits" (Cissy's word) of political gossip. They reviewed books and movies, posed for promotion pictures, searched the District of Columbia for answers to such questions as "Where in this town can you get a good mint julep?" and flirted not only with the President of the United States but with his Cabinet and with members of both Houses of Congress.

"My ravishing little characters," as Cissy called them, wafted more than perfume into the city room. "It is one of the mysterious ways of Allah to make women troublesome when he makes them beautiful," George Bernard Shaw noticed. The most obvious trouble the *Herald's* "lovelies" caused was to the men who ran its city desk. The girls handed in stories at the last minute, missed deadlines while they made up their faces, and squeezed tears from the eyes of veteran copy readers by writing in pencil on the back of cocktail napkins.

"I don't know why these young ladies should get away with such execrable copy," Cissy grumbled. She snarled at them as often as she could muster the strength. Her own judgment about female features and columns, particularly after she acquired some experience, was respected by other editors as astute, if at times bizarre. Having recognized the need for a clubwomen's column, Cissy then pressured her hens to make it readable. "Add the little personal touch," she lectured. "Little adjectives about hair, hats, smiles, voices—a chatty, intimate kind of story as if you *had* really been to those meetings and enjoyed being there." The good club ladies appreciated her effort and made the *Herald* a bulletin board for their activities.

Considering her unfamiliarity with the domestic arts,

Cissy did well enough with features and columns aimed at housewives: the elaborate food layouts, home council advice, gardening tips, and other inducements to patronize the advertisers. She personally wrote a cooking column, using her cook's name, Rebecca, as a by-line, flavoring the recipes with homespun Southern dialect.

Cissy's most successful editorial approach to women readers was not through their kitchens but through their fantasies. She believed that Washington, especially after the Roosevelt Administration expanded the government bureaucracy, was a city which collected emotionally unsatisfied women. Some were wives of the type Alice Roosevelt Longworth characterized with the celebrated quip, "Washington is full of successful men and the women they married a long time ago"; others were party-giving widows and divorcees; most were lonely small-town girls who came to Washington looking for glamour only to discover thousands of other lonely small-town girls and hundreds of married men. Cissy's paper served them glamour and sympathy.

Washington Society was a mine of glamour, laden with rich personalities and glittering entertainments, and it was journalistically untapped save in isolated books and magazine articles. The town's newspapers had treated Society gingerly, tramping on no toes, baring no breasts. Even Hearst's *Herald* and evening *Times* left the *Social Register* in relative peace. Cissy's initial memo on projected changes in the *Herald* mentioned "going after smart society people." Her forty-nine years in Society had given her an appreciation of the common curiosity about "how the better half live." Cats, she said, just love looking at kings. And it doesn't make any difference what SOCI-

ETY does," she explained to her reporters. "Whether they dress up as babies for charity's sweet sake, join in a point-to-point horse race, work at a clam bake, knit socks, go duck shooting, or whatever, they are still SOCIETY and should be so labelled."

It was important for the reader's benefit that names on the Society Page connote faces. In 1930 the *Herald* printed an eight-column photo feature every day for several months on *grandes dames* and debutantes, describing their hobbies and husbands and hairdos. Washington's best Society reporter was hired away from the *Post* to organize the *Herald* Society Section into a public diary of these Social Personalities. The *Herald's* new Society editor, Ruth Jones, had begun her career at the rival *Post* with a scoop on the engagement of Woodrow Wilson's daughter. During her ten years at the *Herald* she wrote under the by-line "Jean Eliot." She was perhaps America's first "society editor" in the modern sense of the word.

As Cissy's *Herald* reported it, Washington Society read like a circus. There were political balancing acts in the main ring, ladies in spangles, amusing sideshows, freaks, clowns and more clowns. New *Herald* columns—"Washington Merry-Go-Round," "The Washington Sideshow," and "These Charming People"—reflected Cissy's latent contempt for social Washington as a "childish place."

Like her brother Joe, who was never prouder than the time a lion tamer invited him to try his skill with a whip and a chair, Cissy was more respectful of real carnivals than social ones. Carney people, she proclaimed, "have guts."

The garish and unwanted publicity that Cissy threw on Old Guard Society did much to kill it off in Washington. As an editor Cissy vastly refined the early attacks she mounted in her novels against the starchy upper crust. From a clumsy swordsman she had become a deft fencer who wounded "with a touch scarcely seen or felt," and let the blood of all her mother had held dear. Such quiet mayhem demanded an intimate knowledge of one's victims, and Cissy knew Society like a leopard knows his jungle. She knew, for example, that her childhood girl friend, Countess Marguerite Cassini, had never been fully accepted by Washington Society even during the Countess' turn-of-the-century heyday as the Russian Embassy hostess. Marguerite "used too much physical charm," the complaint went. Once Theodore Roosevelt had ordered her off limits to Alice. Marguerite was "fast" company for Washington's own debutantes—Helen Hay, Mary Victoria Leiter, "Bessie" Glover, Mathilde Townsend, Josephine Boardman, and, of course, Princess Alice.

By 1937 Marguerite, who had lost her money and position twenty years earlier in the Russian revolution, was plump and gray and poor. Cissy resurrected her in a feature story. She introduced Marguerite as "The Famous Countess Cassini who once had all Washington on its ear." As a follow-up, she hired Marguerite to collaborate with the *Herald* feature department on memoirs. The price was $600 and a reporter's job for her twenty-two-year-old son, Igor. Cissy soothed her old friend's anxiety over the racy tones her wistful memories were taking in the hands of *Herald* feature writers. Soon, "I Lived for Love" rolled off the presses, filled with unfortunate episodes and remarks from the lives of the Countess' old friends. It was calculated to put readers in doubt about the morals of *fin-de-siècle* debutantes. Photographs of

Marguerite when she was young were grouped intimately on the *Herald* pages with photos of Helen Hay, Mary Leiter, Alice Roosevelt, and the other impeccables.

Judging from her erratic behavior, Cissy was never quite certain when she was exploiting friends. She could run to the barricades for them and then, when the crisis was past, think nothing of holding them up to ridicule— particularly if it benefited the *Herald*. Hearing that Evalyn Walsh McLean was about to be scandalized in a *New York Post* series, Cissy raised $100,000 bribery money in one evening. (The payoff wasn't needed, even if one would have been accepted. A *Herald* reporter learned the McLean exposé had been shelved.)

On the other hand a more loyal friend would not have enticed Mrs. McLean to write a newspaper column. Evalyn had proved she couldn't write in her autobiography *Father Struck It Rich* ("We could not buy a colored boy, of course, although it was our habit to buy anything we wanted."). But Cissy savored the delicious amusement of seeing all those malapropisms in her paper. "It seems fantastic," wrote Mrs. McLean in her first column, "that Cissy, who has done so much good and done such wonderful things with her newspaper, would be willing to allow such a waste of space." Of course, it was Cissy who suggested the name for Evalyn's efforts, "My Say," a parody of Eleanor Roosevelt's column, "My Day."

Mrs. McLean was a zany woman, who liked people and entertained them "on a scale never seen before or since in Washington," according to social historian Cleveland Amory. Despite her absurdities, Mrs. McLean was well liked. She was a mother confessor to famous men, including labor leader John L. Lewis, who woke her in the middle of the night when his wife was dying to weep on Mrs. McLean's generous shoulder. It was popularity rather than wealth or intelligence which allowed her to bang a fist on the table during a White House dinner and demand, "Now you listen to Old Lady McLean!"

But Cissy determined in 1936 that it was time for a new Society leader, preferably one created by the *Herald*. With striking presumption Cissy launched a campaign to enthrone a woman little known to anyone except *Herald* advertising executives. Her chosen instrument was Gwendolyn Cafritz, a giddy but intelligent Hungarian with frank social ambitions. Morris Cafritz, her husband, was a self-made real estate tycoon, whose advertising was coveted by the *Herald*. Cissy personally kicked off the campaign, delivering an orchid plant from the Dower House greenhouse to the Cafritzes' modern mansion on Foxhall Road overlooking Glover Park. Abstract pictures, low-slung contemporary furniture, and a built-in nightclub adorned the Cafritz home. At the time Washington Society was amused and mildly shocked by the Cafritzes and their gaudy pleasure dome. But Mrs. Cafritz remembers, "Cissy saw I had potential." Mrs. Cafritz soon justified Cissy's expectations and the splashy copy *Herald* hens wrote about her. "I *always* invite senators," Mrs. Cafritz confided after her installation. "But I seldom play around with the Lower House." As for Mr. Cafritz, he increased advertising in the *Herald* without a word ever having to be said.

Cissy could be partially condoned for pumping fresh blood into the rigid social caste structure of Washington. But even granting such democratic sentiments, Cissy's Svengali act with the Cafritzes remained a self-serving practical joke. It was the kind of inconoclasm that Cissy institutionalized in a Society feature she dubbed "These Charming People." When Cissy pronounced that phrase in her airy drawl, her meaning was clear.

It was over a drink at Chicago's Tavern Club in 1932 that Cissy recruited Martha Blair, a handsome socialite, to author the "Charming People" column. A resident of suburban Lake Forest and recently divorced from William Mitchell Blair, Martha knew little of Washington and few of its social luminaries. But once she was on the job Martha's column picked up. Politicians began reading "These Charming People" for slices of hot political cake layered in with Martha's usual Society frosting. It was uncanny what Martha reported, unless you knew she was dating Arthur Krock, the Washington Bureau Chief of *The New York Times*.

Cissy raised Martha to $100 a week for two columns. When she married Krock, however, the *Times* publisher, Arthur Sulzberger, objected to the piracy of information for which Krock was paid $25,000 a year. Cissy fretted over the loss of Krock's *sub rosa* contributions to "These Charming People." One night, after drinking too much, she telephoned Krock: "Martha's column bores me. I'm sick of her. She's spoiled. She writes about the wrong people."

"Good," answered Krock, eager to put an end to his wife's embarrassing work. Enraged rather than satisfied, Cissy flailed around, searching for a way to get even. She jerked Martha's next column from the *Herald*'s early edition, and then changed her mind and put it back in. The next evening, at a British Embassy party, Cissy berated her old friend Krock about his new wife, until the dignified Timesman firmly called for a halt to the insults. Cissy rose from the dinner table and sailed out of the embassy, leaving behind her ermine wrap. In the morning Martha returned the ermine to Dupont Circle, attaching a polite note of resignation, which Cissy accepted, thus denying her the severance pay due dismissed employees. In retaliation Martha supplied the rival *Post* with free social tips for several days and then announced, "Now that I've got all the vixen out of me, I'm through."

But Cissy wasn't through. She vented her spleen on a young *Time* magazine reporter, Mary Johnson, whose sin was to file the story to her home office. To worsen matters, *Time's* account of the break-up was accompanied by a picture of Cissy which, she growled, "makes me look like a gorilla." Cissy's answer in the *Herald*, a pointless diatribe against Mary Johnson entitled "Henry Luce's Poulette" hurt Cissy much more than it hurt Miss Johnson.

Cissy's excessive and irrational anger was caused by something deeper than simply losing a columnist. She formed strong emotional attachments to the girls who worked at the *Herald* and she struck out against the loosening of those bonds by marriage, changing times, or other events beyond her control. As she sometimes recognized herself, Cissy was seeking a replacement for her daughter, Felicia, from whom she was tragically estranged.* Martha had been one of Felicia's replacements. In addition to her *Herald* duties Cissy had pressed her into service as a super-social secretary. Martha recalls

---

* Felicia married an Englishman in 1934. When Cissy heard the news she complained, "I don't even know the young man—if he is young." The marriage ended in divorce.

planning parties for Cissy with the freedom of a spoiled only child. "I invited my friends, ordered the most expensive wine and food, arranged the flowers, chose the music, then handed over the bills."

Cissy's policy of collecting spirited women—some talented, some aristocratic and many spoiled—created inevitable rivalries in the office. She encouraged friction, perhaps to flatter her aging vanity, though publicly she blessed the competition as good for the *Herald*. To her pets she gave beautiful clothes, some she had never worn. She sent roses from her greenhouse. She singled out certain of them for lunch at Dupont Circle and for trips in her railroad car. She favored them with confidences and sought their confidences in return. Some were hurt badly by Cissy. They allowed themselves to become her creatures, fetching and carrying gossip, feeding her whims, only to be discarded. No girl, however willing or pleasing, could ultimately take Felicia's place. Cissy found something wrong with every one.

As for the male members of her staff, Cissy was distrustful, constantly looking for signs of sabotage. "Men," she wryly observed, "are not at all sensitive about taking a woman's money, but they do not like to work for her. Sometimes a man can be overcome by persuasion, but more often it takes violent methods. Above all, a woman must not let herself be licked." As a female editor-publisher, surrounded by male advisors and assistants, Cissy put too little emphasis on persuasion and too much on violence. Overly intent on not being licked, Cissy had pestered Hearst to give her managing editors who were malleable. Hearst, to conserve his normal control over editorial appointments, had gently dissuaded Cissy when she pleaded for personnel changes. (YOU WOULD NOT WANT THAT EDITOR, he wired Cissy. HE WOULD TURN OUT A GRACEFUL PAPER NOT A STRONG ONE.)

When Cissy sent one managing editor packing because she was unhappy with his manners, Brisbane chided, "You don't get an alligator for its looks or politeness, but for the knobby skin that makes good satchels and shoes. . . . You, especially, could get along with any editor because, to begin with, you could get him completely on your side, and failing that, which seems impossible, you could scare him to death."

Hearst had finally given in and instructed his business managers: "I guess really Mrs. Patterson will have to select her own personnel (with my approval) and handle them in her own way. She is perfectly competent to do so, having such particularly apt talents for handling men!"

George DeWitt, one of Cissy's chosen managing editors, was fired, rehired, and fired again within a four-year period. For one full year Cissy tried doing without a managing editor. Frank Waldrop, a principal editor of the post-Hearst years, held his job till the end, but not without periodic trips through Purgatory. "In every crisis," she stormed at him in 1942, "I have found that you are against me, not for me. I'm working with a series of ignorant, incompetent people." Predictably, Cissy's most compatible editor was a woman, Jackie Martin, who as head of the photo department had eight men under her.

Brisbane attempted to sneak some sense into Cissy's head about handling lower-rung employees, but as with his advice on editors, it was appreciated but not followed. "If I have had any success as an editor," he counseled, "it

has been to always work through department heads."
Cissy had trouble learning that reporters could not be
treated like her domestic servants and she never understood channels. When she wanted something, she went to
the source. Edward Folliard, later a top political reporter
on the *Post,* was called into Cissy's office in 1932 and
blandly told to write a scoop every day for page one.
Another young reporter called to the inner sanctum was
fired without explanation or even so much as a look from
Cissy, who was having her hair done at the time. A third
reporter was invited by Cissy to have a drink with her.
Later on, back at the office, she thought he was tipsy and
fired him. But her generosity was as unpredictable as her
anger. When told that he had a one-drink capacity, she
hired him back, with a raise. A *Herald* newsman caught in
an alcoholic spiral was dismissed, but his wife was hired
as a secretary and he was put on Cissy's private pension
list until he found other work.

Cissy was constantly lending money to staffmen with
unexpected medical bills, sending flowers, and giving
parties for her reporters. But her impulsive generosity
didn't extend to the more orderly and businesslike largesse of granting periodic raises and allowing for vaca-
tions. A crimp was put into her erratic and frightening
maternalism after the Newspaper Guild won bargaining
rights at the *Herald* in 1937.

The most startling male reporter on the *Herald* staff
was one Cissy recruited herself. She hand-picked Marguerite Cassini's son, Igor, to replace Martha Krock, and
Igor caused as much initial consternation in the city room
as any of Cissy's hens ever had. He appeared immature,
overly sensitive, and "foreign." "Mrs. Patterson hired the

worst creeps!" an ex-copy boy recalls. But, surprisingly, Igor was a hustler. One reader remembers he read Cassini for the same reason he scanned the obituary page—to see which of his friends were "dead" that day. By June, 1939, when Igor was only twenty-four years old, he had enough notches in his column to be Washington Society's number-one enemy. Like Cissy, Igor was impervious to what Society thought about him and paid little attention to the occasional threats.

Thus it was that Igor walked into a country club dance at Warrenton, Virginia, and asked for a dance with a girl whose reputation he had previously tarnished in his column. A club attendant interrupted to ask Igor outside, where someone had supposedly smashed his automobile. The girl's brother and four other gentleman hotbloods from the Virginia hunt country were waiting for him. They choked him, beat him over the head with a flashlight, drove him to a deserted spot where they stripped, tarred, feathered, and left him.

"As objectively as a reporter who has been taken for a ride can write, these are the facts of what happened to Igor Cassini," he wrote in his column "Petit Point." For further enlightenment, a picture showed Igor wearing his feathers. Igor knew a good story when he saw one. So did the *Herald*'s Cissy, who ran it on page one.

10

The Nasty Details

Throughout her career as a Hearst editor Cissy deftly "coped with" the ménage of Hearst executives who traveled the circuit checking the Chief's properties. The lesser powers among them, including managing editors, she simply short-circuited. But when the moneymen came around to check the books, the circulation, and the advertising, Cissy squealed. She aired her annoyance at the inquisitive Hearst executives in a flurry of letters and telegrams to Brisbane and Hearst. Feminine wiles decorated her pique. She inserted her digs between glowing progress reports on the *Herald* and compliments to the Chief. One regional circulation executive she dismissed as "a regular old Shylock. Ain't he awful?" She characterized the Washington circulation director as "slow-talking and somewhat tricky." When Colonel Frank Knox, a prestigious Pooh-bah in the Organization at the time, ordered economies in the *Herald* operation, the Chief promptly received a Cissy missile. Knox, she complained, was a man who came to dinner bearing a "dripping axe." But Cissy eventually defanged the plenipotentiaries: "Darling Tawm" White, "Walter Dear" Howey, "Dearest Artie" Brisbane, "My Favorite Colonel" Knox, "Beloved W.R." Hearst and all.

The elderly Brisbane was her Sugar Daddy in the Organization; she flattered, scolded, vamped, and exploited him as shamelessly as she had coaxed "extra pennies" from her own father thirty years before. There seemed no limit to the favors Cissy asked of him—editorial judgements, personal consolation, even promotional appearances for the *Herald*. "I am going to ask that the Society of Jewish Women come to my house to tea on October eighteenth. If you are to be in town on that day will you not address these ladies? Just a few graceful remarks will do."

She lured Brisbane to Washington to give pep talks to the *Herald* staff and to impress *Herald* advertisers over champagne at her mansion. He benignly indulged Cissy, but not without an occasional tug at the reins. "A.B. says I must not harass him and I try not to," Cissy wrote Hearst. She sent him affectionate presents, subscribed to his favorite charities, gave his daughter a coming-out party at Dupont Circle, and kept a room for him in her house. A butler had standing orders to watch Brisbane when he went out to make sure he had on all his clothes. Cissy's secretary recalled that Brisbane had once absentmindedly dictated his "Today" column to her without his pants on. When Brisbane wished to resolve a tiff with Louisiana's Senator Long, Cissy arranged a dinner at Dupont Circle.

She lavished similar largesse on Hearst. Once, when W.R. was planning a trip from New York to Washington,

Cissy sent up her private railroad car, the chintz boudoir, to transport him, at a cost of $2,700. On one occasion she and Brisbane presented Hearst with a twelve-cylinder touring Cadillac. Another time, she played to Hearst's unquenchable taste for art works with an Italian Primitive madonna by Segna di Bonaventure, which was worth $20,000.

Hearst also singled Cissy out for special treatment. On one of her trips West her private railroad car was met at San Simeon by a brass band. The Chief was intrigued by Cissy's style—her gall, her sparkle, her extravagance—as much as he was impressed by her newspaper connections. Sometimes Cissy complained that Hearst had hired her not as an editor but as an ornament. Repeatedly he suggested that she leave her boring work at the office to join his court in California or on trips abroad. Most of his employees considered such invitations command performances, but Cissy invented a delightful series of excuses to turn Hearst down ("the doctors say I have tuberculosis"). It tickled W.R. that every time Cissy came West in the chintz boudoir, the trip cost more than her annual salary.

Hearst and Cissy conducted their business affairs through Western Union. Both were heavy travelers, but their secretaries knew how to keep the dialogue flowing between Washington and California, Miami and Munich, New York and Paris. Their telegrams were baroque and more expensive than necessary. The amount of flattery Hearst and Cissy exchanged was slightly more than the amount of business they concluded. I APPROVE OF EVERYTHING YOU DO WHETHER YOU RAISE THE RATES OR RAISE THE DICKENS WITH US, one Hearst wire read. In the beginning, while Cissy was discovering the newspaper world, she had constant inspirations, but not all of them were as original as she supposed. Hearst cherished enthusiasm and tried not to squelch it, and thus he paid close attention to the explosion of telegrams which followed Cissy's discoveries. He usually answered Cissy's wires within twenty-four hours. And more often than not his answer would open with a fanfare of flattery, slide gracefully and almost incidentally to a rejection of Cissy's brainstorm, then close on a note of renewed esteem.

For example, on the last day of March, 1931, it came to Cissy that the *Herald* could get a jump on the rival *Post* by moving up deadline time and thus getting on the streets first with a newspaper. Hearst's April Fool's Day reply included the obvious conclusion that the *Post* would match the earlier deadline and nothing would be gained—except the expenses of change.

Cissy and Hearst whipped off telegrams and letters at odd moments. One Hearst note, in black crayon, was written on a San Simeon lunch menu, the sentences carefully laced around the day's offering of Strained Gumbo, Hungarian Szegedi, and Chinese Cabbage. The telegram was a dangerous medium of communication for Cissy. She sometimes scribbled out her momentary anger impulsively and sent it westward before a calmer head prevailed. Often, Hearst was amused by her tart tongue. Occasionally he was taken aback.

In September, 1932, when Cissy was trying to increase advertising in the *Herald*'s weekly food supplement, she ran up against the Organization's rule that national food advertising was handled by a national Hearst selling staff. Ad salesmen for individual Hearst papers could call on the big food chains and national brand producers, but they weren't permitted to take orders.

. . . WE MIGHT AS WELL SEND A COUPLE OF PHONO-GRAPH RECORDS AROUND THE COUNTRY, Cissy wired Hearst. HOPING OUR OWN MEN MAY BE GIVEN THE SELL-ING RESPONSIBILITY. WON'T YOU PLEASE AS A FAVOR AN-SWER ME DIRECT.

Hearst's answer a day later was uncharacteristically brief and bald: ALL RIGHT, WE WILL INSIST ON ALLOW-ING YOUR FOOD SOLICITORS TO SIGN.

Cissy was a magnanimous victor: SOMEDAY YOU WILL HAVE TO SAY NO TO ME BUT I AM GLAD IT WASN'T THIS TIME BECAUSE WE ARE GOING TO GO OUT AND MAKE A GREAT SUCCESS FOR YOU STOP I UNDERSTAND THE GRAPE SEASON IS THE MOST BEAUTIFUL OF ALL IN CALIFORNIA.

Occasionally Cissy struck the latent dynamite in Hearst. In the spring of 1935, while arguing with Tom White over renewing a society editor's contract, she wired White and sent a copy to Hearst:

I CANNOT UNDERSTAND WHY IT OCCURRED TO YOU TO HAMSTRING A HEALTHY GROWING AND INCREASINGLY POPULAR PROPERTY WHEN YOU HAVE SO MANY CORPSES LYING AROUND TO PLAY WITH. The next morning an an-swer from W.R. awaited Cissy at the *Herald* office, and it fairly burned the lacquer off her antique desk. NOW SISTER, warned the Chief, WHY GET SARCASTIC JUST BE-CAUSE TOM WHITE IS TRYING TO TEMPER THE WIND TO THE SHORN LAMB.

In Hearst's imagery, Cissy was the raging wind and he the sacrificial lamb. He knew better and so did Cissy. Despite her bravado, Cissy feared the tall titan with the pink flesh, the little ice-blue eyes, and the soft high voice which was never raised in anger. W.R. could "fix" her and Cissy respected him for that, according to her daughter. And Cissy thought Hearst a newspaper genius. Felicia says her mother was uncritically worshipful of Chief Hearst. He occupied a seat at the right hand of brother Joe in Cissy's pantheon of heroes.

"Joe Patterson says you are the greatest newspaper genius the world has ever known," she wrote in 1935. "I would love you for this reason if for none other. . . . I think I would love you anyhow. I love you."

When slapped on the wrist by the genius, Cissy cried her contrition. The "NOW SISTER" telegram drew an agonizing apology from her which ended, "I read every word you send me with a great big magnifying glass, so please don't you be sarcastic either." Hearst was just as glad to see the storm clouds roll over. He was too courtly a man to spat comfortably with ladies. Indeed, Hearst's excessive courtesy permeated his business relationship with Cissy, which was conducted rather like a Japanese tea ceremony. The Chief's telegrams would arrive, gloating over the success of makeup changes or new features added to the *Los Angeles Examiner*, the *New York American* or another of Hearst's favorite papers. I MERELY ADVISE THAT YOUR EDITORIAL PAGES WOULD LOOK BETTER WITH THE MAKEUP WE HAVE TRIED OUT WITH SOME SUCCESS IN LOS ANGELES, a wire to Cissy read on April 11, 1935. Cissy knew the rules and she took the advice as an order. The changes, she wired back, made a big difference, and *Herald* readers were taking to them like fish to water.

Hearst preferred his own editorial ideas to others' and he assumed that what interested readers in one city would be of equal interest in all other cities. When, in 1932, he raved to Cissy about the *New York American's* treatment of the page opposite the editorial page, Cissy dutifully laid out her comparable page with the same features and by-lined columnists, but she was none too pleased with the results. The editorial page and its mate, facing each other in the center of the newspaper, were so different in style, she said, that they looked like a "person with a galosh on one foot and a dancing pump on the other," a remark which got back to Hearst and did not amuse him.

Occasionally Cissy did Hearst personal favors in her newspaper without him having to ask. In 1935, when Marion Davies' movie *Miss Glory* was playing in Washington, the *Herald* ran a serial of the story on its drama page. The circulation department pitched into the promotional effort, distributing thirty thousand *Miss Glory* pamphlets.

The budgetary requirements of carrying Hearst's canned features, columnists, and news wire services were heavy. Cissy wasn't much concerned that the paper was top-heavy with features and low on news reporters. She thought features more interesting to the average reader, but she wanted Washington features, commissioned by Cissy not Hearst.

Some, but not all, of her attempts to change the pattern gained a grudging acceptance as she gained in experience. Fiction, Cissy recommended (thinking of her women readers again), would make a nice change of pace from the columns of heavy news in a morning paper. "I suggest omitting fiction for a while and seeing what happens," Hearst counseled, remarking that even at its best, fiction had only semi-news quality. The "a while" became permanent.

Despite the many advisories from the Chief, Cissy had

some success in the middle thirties making over the *Herald*'s heavy black headlines and sensation play that were the trademarks of the Hearst papers. By 1936 Cissy's *Herald*, with thinner type and more sophisticated makeup, looked smarter and lighter than its sister *Times*. Cissy also encouraged some photographic experiments, first with debutante parties and then with still life for the food section, her special pet.

Cissy constantly complained that the tired old makeup editors she inherited were sloppy and tasteless. She fired several for running a story about Gen. Douglas Mac-Arthur alongside "floating kidney, laxative and dandruff ads." Cissy toyed with makeup gimmicks like putting a stars-and-stripes border around the front page on Washington's birthday. But one thing Cissy did not give the face of her paper was dignity. She lacked the resources and the inclination. Brisbane knew that in Washington it was a serious fault, perhaps fatal. The *Post*, he warned in 1935, "takes on the appearance of a solid, substantial, dignified morning paper. There is something in dignity, even in intentional *heaviness*."

Cissy was a walking promotion for the *Herald,* which was fortunate because, as she said, the newspaper's promotion department "ain't." Her own lavish style of living and friendships with famous people were not overlooked. Sometimes Cissy used her private assets for a specific promotional stunt. The most successful was the Golden Mirror contest. It began with a quip by Columnist Walter Winchell that there were no pretty girls in Washington. The *Herald* set out to prove him wrong and called on all patriotic and pretty young women in the capital to send their photographs to the newspaper. An annual judging was held at Cissy's Maryland country estate, Dower House, with such Society figures as Evalyn McLean and Gwen Cafritz making the selections. The winners, known as Golden Mirror girls, were treated to an elaborate dance at Dupont Circle. The promotion proved so successful that it was continued during the war, when the Golden Mirror girls were queens for a night at USO dances.

But the *Herald*'s brightest promotional property remained Cissy herself, and consequently her engagement calendar was always filled with appearances, speeches, and radio talks. "My speech before the Jewish Society yesterday was a great success," she wrote Brisbane on May 9, 1932. "The chairman made a speech in praise of the retiring president. Everybody cried. The retiring president made a speech in praise of the new president. Everybody cried. The toastmistress proposed a moment of silence in memory of a defunct member. Everybody cried. I made a most touching speech about intermarriage between the Jews and the Christians, and everybody cried. This time I cried too."

When it came to advertising, Cissy was so shameless a huckster that *The New York Times* was later to mention it in her obituary. The paper badly needed more advertisements and Cissy wanted to be its secret weapon in the competition for the ad dollar. Brisbane, never one to look practicality in the mouth, bluntly counseled her, "Get out those blacksmith diamond bracelets, get out that smile that would melt the rock of Gibralter and *cultivate the advertisers.*"

"I may be imprudent mentioning your great fortune," he wrote on another occasion, "however, it insures respect

in the Washington advertiser which is what you want."
Taking her cue, Cissy played to the social aspirations
of advertisers and would-be advertisers by adding their
names to the guest lists for Dupont Circle parties. "Disgusted" by "all the nasty little truss ads," she approached
the prestige merchants whom she had patronized heavily
for years. Her dressmaker, florist, caterer, hairdresser, and
grocer felt obliged to oblige her. She wrote personal letters to her friends, the presidents of companies, and re-
warded them by improving the display of *Herald* advertising and the quality of reproduction.

The *Herald* competed for advertising as much if not
more against the *Times* as against the other three Washington newspapers. The competition was cutthroat and
the two Hearst papers constantly slew each other before
prospective advertisers. Each paper had its separate pipe-
lines to the Hearst executive offices in New York. Con-
spiracies were born like rabbits. "You needed a ouija
board to figure out the snarls the Hearst Organization
created for itself," William Shelton recalls of his days as
Cissy's business manager. Similar fraternal rivalries were
confounding Hearst's profit sheets in every city in which
he owned morning and afternoon newspapers. Determined to lessen the destructive competition, the Chief
wrote a general letter to all executives in February, 1933,
calling for a cease-fire between the A.M.s and P.M.s.

"This is one of the most important letters I have ever
written," Hearst began ominously. He then announced
the formation of a national committee and local commit-
tees in each city to screen promotional and advertising
copy against unnecessarily disparaging remarks.

Hearst papers, the Chief's edicts notwithstanding, also

fought A.M. against P.M. for circulation. In Washington, Hearst ordered that preference be given to the *Times* on most matters, including circulation budgets, because it competed against *The Evening Star,* the biggest and most prosperous Washington paper of the 1930s. From the day Cissy began at the *Herald* she complained to executives in New York and to Hearst in California about this policy. She repeatedly reminded them that the *Herald* was succeeding in spite of them, not because of them. With each perceptible rise in *Herald* circulation she dispatched a telegram. On October 11, 1931, she wired Hearst: WE ARE RUNNING REFINED BUT SENSATIONAL FRONT-PAGE STREAMER TOMORROW MORNING AND FOREVER AFTER QUOTE LARGEST MORNING CIRCULATION IN THE NATIONS CAPITAL. In time, Cissy surreptitiously won William Shelton, then directing circulation for both of Hearst's Washington papers, to her cause. Without Hearst's knowledge Shelton switched allegiance from the *Times* to the *Herald,* going so far as to juggle figures to boost Cissy's circulation. Between 1930 and 1936 the *Herald* circulation doubled to nearly a hundred thousand—or so Shelton's records said.

The Depression staggered the huge Hearst organization of newspapers, magazines, wire services, and such unrelated enterprises as real estate and movies. The money tree was beginning to wither, blighted with debts that creditors no longer willingly assumed. The Chief, always the optimist, couldn't admit that the nation's economic collapse was anything but a passing phenomenon. But as the months passed and as the national indicators of economic health pointed down and still downward, he reluctantly instituted economy measures. A first step was to separate himself, at least publicly, from the financial decisions. Hearst's editorial and organizational skill had never extended to money matters but such deficiencies were relatively harmless until the Depression. Partly to ease the clamor of creditors, Hearst set up an executive and finance committee of seven top executives in October of 1930. "Their authority is absolute," he wrote to all publishers of Hearst newspapers. In fact the committee's vaunted authority stopped with the Chief. He continued to enjoy his stupendous personal expenditures, estimated at $15,000,000 annually.

The world-wide pinch continued, despite Hearst's optimistic forecast to Cissy that the election of Roosevelt would lead to substantial improvement within several months. The economy message traveled down the line in the Hearst Organization, reaching the city rooms of his papers in 1934 and 1935. In Chicago fourteen top reporters on the newly combined *Herald-Examiner* saw their $100 and $200 salaries reduced to $60 a week, the new maximum. Similar reductions were instituted in Washington. Cissy seized the occasion to comfort the harried Hearst: I THINK YOU MIND THE CUT MORE THAN ANY-BODY STOP OUR WHOLE OFFICE HAS TAKEN IT PHILO-SOPHICALLY EVEN GAILY STOP THEY SAY THEY ARE GLAD TO HAVE THEIR JOBS. She renounced her own $15,000 salary, gaining independence and incidentally aiding the crumbling organization.

Cissy had been chafing under Hearst's velvet thumb. Several times she had attempted to coax him into selling, renting, or lending her the *Herald*. By November, 1936, Cissy wrote Hearst that she was seriously considering quitting. She confessed, "the truth is that for many months now I have been working without real interest or real energy. . . . I used to feel keen as mustard at the office, and now I feel like a dreary old woman, anxious to quit.

"No—nobody has treated me rough. Nobody has crossed me. Nobody has been unkind. In fact, you all seem to have banded together to spoil the life out of me, and turn my head. My only criticism is, of course, you have been—and here is a real criticism—too indulgent. And how I loved it! The six and a half years I have spent working for you have been worth more to me than all the rest of my life put together."

Edged in, almost as an afterthought, Cissy expressed doubt that she could have "accomplished anything of value if you had turned over the *Herald* one way or the other to me."

Cissy's poor-mouthing wasn't to be taken seriously. Within a year she was leasing the *Herald* and within another eighteen months she owned the paper, a chain of events for which Cissy could thank the Depression and not Hearst who clung to his offspring to the end. The *Herald* and its afternoon sister the *Times* were ripped from him by a second "conservation committee"—this one with full control—appointed in 1936 to stave off bankruptcy of the Hearst empire. Headed by Hearst's old friend, lawyer Clarence Shearn, the seven-man committee had complete authority to liquidate losing properties, reorganize the ninety-four separate Hearst enterprises, even control the Chief's personal spending. Hearst retained editorial control only so long as his orders didn't conflict with budgetary ceilings set by the committee. He had submitted to the shearing of his powers only when it became apparent that nothing less would satisfy the creditors holding the $126,000,000 Hearst debt.

The *Herald* was the kind of newspaper Hearst could no longer afford. By 1936 it was losing $1,115,933 annually; it had lost some $13,000,000 since 1920. The lease, which called for Cissy to assume part of the yearly loss, cost Cissy $1,000,000. That was a lot for a losing property in the Depression. Hearst knew it and was grateful. After the deluge passed, he often liked to say, a bit expansively, that Cissy and Marion Davies saved him by each contributing a million.

Cissy's assistance was not quite as generous as it appeared on the surface. The arrangement called for Cissy to lend Hearst the million and lease the *Herald*. (Five months later the *Times* was thrown into the deal.) She borrowed the money from the Morgan Guaranty Bank and charged Hearst 5.5 per cent interest, which was more than she was paying the bank. In addition the loan was to go toward the purchase price if Cissy ever bought the Washington papers outright. The shrewd business deal was closed by Tom White.

Still, Cissy's $1,000,000 was a better alternative for Hearst than that offered by Eugene Meyer, publisher of the competing *Post*. As Cissy later unraveled it to her staff: "It came to the point where Mr. Meyer offered $650,000 or at any rate over $600,000 for the *Herald*, and on the sixth of August, the *Herald* was all but signed, sealed and delivered to Mr. Meyer. You can't blame him for that . . . it was an excellent deal for him, but it meant the paper would go out of existence. I called Mr. Hearst at three in the morning and commenced to cry on the phone and I said—I don't know what I said—but I couldn't bear to have the *Herald* go out of business. And he said, 'Well, Cissy, you tell me what you want to do and I will tell my folks to do it.'

"And in the morning, because they had to have the money, I went to the bank and borrowed a million dollars, and I made that loan to the Hearst Company. And in that way I was able to take over the lease of the *Herald, Times,* and Sunday [*Times*], and to save the *Herald.*"

During the eighteen months Cissy leased the papers she lost more than $1,000,000. It came to the point where she couldn't afford it. "At the end of the year I would have nothing. My income couldn't begin to cover it," she recorded in a report to her staff. "I talked to my brother, whose opinion I respect more than anybody's. He told me I was a fool to try this thing which had never been a success. . . . Mr. Hearst called over the phone and said I was putting a burden on myself I couldn't carry. Under the lease I had the right to turn the papers back with three months' notice and I also had the right to call my loan. Now I am not trying to be noble—I am more stupid and stubborn—I could have called my loan—*but I did not want to.*"

Instead, Cissy dipped into capital for another $500,000 and acquired sole ownership of the *Herald* and the *Times.* Within a month Cissy announced the two papers were to be merged into a ten-edition, round-the-clock operation. Though she dropped only thirty-seven members of the editorial staff, her employees felt bitter and accused her of throwing people out of jobs. Agitation for a strike followed, and when Cissy heard the news, she called a meeting of her editorial staff and of all department heads. She looked exhausted and broken. "What do you want me to do?" she asked in a low voice, leaning wearily on a table. She documented the staggering costs of duplication and concluded:

"I haven't come here to apologize for anything because I have done the very best I could to keep these papers as they were and I cannot do it—that is all I have to say to you. I couldn't keep two papers because it isn't within the power of my somewhat limited bank account." Cissy left the room alone. Some of her audience were in tears but within twenty-four hours the Newspaper Guild had called a strike meeting.

"There will be no strike," she threatened when a reporter found her at home eating dinner. "If they picket, they'll picket against an empty building. I'll close shop." The Guild took her at her word and called off strike plans. But Cissy's surgery left tension and bitterness in the city room which once had been unusually gay. Newsmen were divided and angry at each other as well as at their new publisher. One faction accused the Guild of attempting to wreck the paper for principle, while another faction charged fair-weather friends with deserting the new and weak union. And there was bitterness against Cissy in the mechanical departments. At one point she asked friends in the F.B.I. to help her catch the typesetter who printed an obscene insult about the publisher in the classified section.

Putting out a newspaper twenty-four hours a day was unbelievably chaotic. It was difficult to plan ahead or maintain quality control with the office staff constantly up against deadlines. The morning and afternoon editions competed for part of the same market, and advertisers created a host of new problems. At one point the city editors of the A.M. and P.M. editions simultaneously quit out of disgust. One harried executive city editor subsequently tried vainly to oversee both operations.

With time the problems proved more manageable and the benefits of a combined operation began to be felt. Features, comics, society, the picture page, and the women's pages were carried unchanged throughout the entire run. The editorial staff was pared down, the business offices were reduced substantially by eliminating duplicate jobs, and manpower was decreased in the mechanical departments by limiting the number of columns set and the number of replate editions. Two sections were carved out of the Sunday paper, the financial stock tables were discontinued, and the Saturday editions were eliminated entirely.

The economies were a welcome tonic and by 1939 the yearly deficit was down to $732,000 from the all-time high of $1,368,024 in 1935. In 1941 Cissy reported "a few dashes of black ink were appearing on the ledger," but not enough; by 1942 the annual loss was $378,822. The break came in 1943, when the *Times-Herald* reported its first profit—$44,152. Cissy immediately took $38,000 of it and lavished bonuses on her staff.

The wartime economy and the public's thirst for combat news helped put Cissy's paper in the black, just as it played a key role in the revival of what was left of Hearst's newspaper empire. Once the corner was turned, Cissy's newspaper profits rose swiftly to $1,000,000 a year. But the satisfaction of making money for a change and the powers of ownership were more than matched by problems and responsibilities. Cissy had been right three years earlier when she told Hearst that the six and a half years she spent as his editor were her happiest. Once she was her own boss, Frank Waldrop, observed "she discovered what it was like to make decisions and have to live by them with no one else to take the consequences, of risking real money for the first time in her life and of being exposed to the world in a situation that could end in disaster."

11

Strange Bedfellows

It was the newspaper business that made Cissy politically conscious and thus, in a political sense, Franklin D. Roosevelt was the only President she ever knew. She was fifty when FDR was inaugurated, but she wrote of the memorable day with the excitement of a fresh experience. Sitting in the grandstands along the inaugural parade route awaiting Roosevelt's arrival "was not unlike waiting for the birth of a child," she exclaimed.

At that writing Cissy had been an editor for less than two years, most of which time had been an intensive cram course in newspaper fundamentals. The coming of the Presidential election year took Cissy to political conventions, and not just as a frivolous female spectator, but as a working editor. Candidate Roosevelt, who knew Cissy on a first-name basis, invited her, at Arthur Brisbane's suggestion, to Hyde Park for a luncheon during his campaign. Cissy came away from the encounter with the impression of a man larger than life, "clearskinned, cleareyed, with athlete's shoulders and a deep chest." She was even impressed with his six-foot-two-inch stature, despite the leg braces he wore as a result of polio.

When Hearst endorsed the Democratic candidate after years as a Republican, Cissy wrote him expansively: "I am so glad that Jesus loves me and that you have come out for the Democrats. . . . It makes life simple, gay and a whole lot more interesting around the office."

On inauguration day her personal *Herald* editorial went all the way for Roosevelt. "Why shy away from the word dictatorship? I don't want to sound as if I were getting exalted or anything, but surely there is a special radiance about this man which makes you feel better just to be around him. A bonnie frank manner. A high spirit. A natural warmth and subtle understanding."

For what appeared more serious reasons, brother Joe, long an enemy of the party of Woodrow Wilson, also was hitching his *New York Daily News* to Roosevelt. Convinced that continued depression would lead to revolution, Patterson made an extraordinary leap of faith and pledged the *News* to back the President's policies for a period of one year. The other publishing member of the family, Bert McCormick, was also invited to Hyde Park. But his meeting with fellow Grotonian Roosevelt failed to spark a similar electricity. "Could Bertie be turned Democratic?" Brisbane queried Cissy—but he knew the answer, "No, not possibly."

Thus, as the Roosevelt era opened, the Patterson-McCormick tribe split fundamentally over what was best for the future of America. Twelve and a half years later, when the Roosevelt era ended, the three would be in bitter harmony over what had been bad for America in the intervening years.

The tribal political split, however short-lived, was the only one—excepting Joe's youthful socialism—since the family patriarch, Joseph Medill, had helped structure the Republican Party. Cissy, Joe, and Bertie were all reared in the tradition of distrust for Great Britain, Wall Street financiers, and the Atlantic Seaboard in general. Their political godfather was Theodore Roosevelt, the trust buster, the conservationist, the defender of a bygone morality, and the aggressive nationalist who defended American interests with a big stick. From this heritage emerged three strikingly different offspring—Joe, the polo-playing proletarian; Bertie, the conservative aristocrat; and Cissy, the worldly hostess, who liked colorful politicans more than political issues.

Joe had been the despair of his family since his Yale days, when Cissy complained that he affected "antediluvian" clothes and chewed wads of gum about the size of eggs. He had advocated socialism during his twenties and, further "betraying his class," published a tabloid that spoke like and for the masses. Not even his valet could prevent Patterson from looking as if his suits were bought on the Bowery.

Bertie adhered to the old mold, living the life of the landed gentry and braying against those who tampered with the turn-of-the-century pattern of American life.

Cissy, though she moved easily in the world of Washington, lacked the political sensitivity of her brother and her cousin. "We women like to pretend we're interested in issues," she confided once, "but really we're interested in personalities."

During the 1920s her natural female interests and her family heritage had blended nicely. For the most colorful men then in the capital were the spiritual sons of TR's Bull Moose Party, the rough, virile, and powerful senators from west of the Appalachians—Walsh and Wheeler of Montana, Johnson of California, Borah of Idaho, and LaFollette of Wisconsin. Crossing party lines, they formed a progressive coalition which wielded power to swing key congressional votes. Their personalities dominated Washington in an era of lackluster Presidents.

A mistress of the fashionable sport of political lion-hunting, Cissy lured the shaggy senators to her Dupont Circle salon, where they confided to her their vanities and intrigues. Then, in the early New Deal, she updated her salon; so many of Roosevelt's wilder followers filtered in and out of Dupont Circle that one magazine referred to it as "Cissy's' pink parlor." In fact she consistently quarreled with communist sympathizers and if she invited some to her house, it was only because she always invited controversy.

Cissy had been fervently anticommunist since her days as a Polish countess, when she had witnessed the fearsome specter of rioting peasants. Like Hearst, Cissy worried about the rise of the Communist Party in the United States. Hearst declared that the New Deal was packed with Reds and he put his syndicated reporters to work to prove the point. Cissy's paper dutifully printed the Hearst alarms. A sensational series "exposing" the teaching of communism at WPA projects in the South ran prominently in the *Herald*.

Serving two masters was difficult and became more so when, in 1934, Hearst declared war on the New Deal. Toward the end of FDR's first term Cissy, disillusioned by Hearst's shrill editorial tirades, confessed to her friend

Harold Ickes that her publisher seemed a little unscrupulous. Gingerly she tried nudging Hearst away from his extreme positions, but she never directly expressed political differences with her awesomely opinionated publisher. Once she did jerk a Hearst-written editorial from the *Herald*. But, conscious of her place, she rationed such tampering practices.

Cissy's Hearst association diminished her value as a Roosevelt ally and, in part, explained why the President was cool and standoffish in his relations with her. FDR was scarcely warmer toward Joe Patterson, his strongest supporter among major newspaper publishers. Roosevelt had seen little of the Pattersons since the Wilson Administration, when he was Assistant Secretary of the Navy. But he remembered that Cissy had been a prominent member of the Anti-Wilson Republicans in Washington, and Patterson, then helping to run the *Tribune,* was a leading opponent of the League of Nations. The President seemed to expect that his Patterson allies would eventually return to the other side of the political fence. Toward Colonel McCormick, Roosevelt felt no ambiguity. From the beginning McCormick was the New Deal's chief press antagonist.

Even in 1932 the *Tribune* publisher had attributed diabolical motives to his fellow Grotonian. By the 1936 campaign McCormick editorialized: "If we want a Cheka* in America, we can and will have one by re-electing Franklin D. Roosevelt and a Congress he can dominate." During the campaign *Tribune* switchboard operators remonstrated with callers that only so many days

* Soviet secret police committee operating against counter-revolutionary movements.

remained "to save America—vote Republican." And in 1936 the *Tribune* news columns included a story head-lined:

ROOSEVELT AREA
IN WISCONSIN IS
HOTBED OF VICE

As the 1936 election approached Cissy admitted she was in a muddle. The New Deal alphabet-soup legislation was not to her taste, certainly not what she had expected in 1932. Her old Republican allegiances were tempted by the regrouped GOP forces, loudly preparing to battle Roosevelt and his New Deal. On the other hand, brother Joe was sticking with FDR. Patterson gave $20,000, the largest single contribution, to FDR's 1936 War Chest.

During the Christmas season Cissy took Hearst from New York to California as a passenger in her "chintz boudoir," stopping off in Kansas for a front-porch visit with Governor Alf Landon, the Republican Presidential hopeful. Hearst came away from the meeting believing Landon should be the next President. Cissy tactfully agreed. "He is just the solid, common type of man we need in the White House." That remark contained all of Cissy's growing uneasiness about Roosevelt who, she felt, was neither solid nor common.

The election months coincided with the end of Cissy's Hearst period. As she took control the *Herald* and the *Times* lost their Hearstian appearance and took on the tribal look. From the *Tribune* Cissy happily bought fea-tures and by-line news stories to bolster the *Times-Herald*. But for opinions and editorial guidance she moved further under the influence of her brother. "Bourbon Bertie," she sniffed, "has the finest mind of the thirteenth century." Following brother Joe's lead, not without misgivings, Cissy privately supported Roosevelt in 1936. Publicly she sat on the fence. In August, 1937, *Time* Magazine characterized her as having "no ax to grind, pro or con New Deal, though leaning more to the liberalism of her brother than to Hearst."

But it was a time to try the allegiances of all but the most loyal FDR followers. Soon after his landslide victory Roosevelt began to dissipate his mandate with alarming speed. Both liberals and conservatives were up in arms over his attempt to pack the Supreme Court. The business community was clamoring about his failure to stem a new economic recession and his initiation of new trust-busting measures. And Americans of every political stripe were nervous about the seriousness of Roosevelt's commitments to neutrality. Within Congress, supposedly controlled by the President, there was an anti-Roosevelt revolution brewing. FDR was pressuring for emergency legislation to cope with the domestic crisis and, impatient with congressional stalling, he was lighting fires under the conservatives in his own party—anticipating the notorious autumn election "purge."

By the summer of 1938 a public opinion poll purported to show that of every two persons who had voted for Roosevelt in 1936, one was regretting it. And an estimated 85 per cent of the nation's newspaper publishers were anti-Roosevelt. At his 487th press conference, on August 23, Roosevelt wryly observed that Patterson's *Daily News* was the only large-circulation paper in the country still supporting the New Deal. Cissy moved to the far outskirts of the President's camp—though she announced no formal break for several years. "I have given Roosevelt every chance," she asserted with exasperation in the spring of 1938. What followed in the *Times-Herald* was no broadside attack on the Roosevelt political structure but a series of snipes.

Among Cissy's complaints against the President was what she considered his arrogant treatment of some of her oldest political friends. Roosevelt's blacklist expanded to include such Senate warhorses as Burton K. Wheeler, Hiram Johnson, Henrik Shipstead, George Norris, and Millard Tydings.

And Cissy felt the President was treading on the dignity of the press. The gay and charming Roosevelt had become a trifle surly at press conferences, baring resentments and treating some reporters like naughty children. At one press conference the President berated a newsman for thirty minutes, charging him and his colleagues with misinterpreting the purpose of a politician's visit to the White House. At a party in the spring of 1938, while Congress was in the process of rejecting his wage-hours act, Cissy asked him how he intended to regain the confidence of the American people. "Well, Cissy," he snapped, "what would *you* do?"

Cissy answered Roosevelt's facetious question with an open letter in her newspaper on April 10, 1938, two days after the President's most humiliating congressional defeat. She timed her letter to coincide with an important convention of power in Washington, the Gridiron Dinner, an annual event given by the male brahmins of the Washington press corps and attended by America's most prestigious editors, publishers, and politicians. In the course of perusing the Washington papers, the visiting moguls read Cissy's editorial explaining that an angry Roosevelt had asked her how she would cope with his dilemma. Cissy impudently began: "Dear Mr. President:"

> If you will do this, Mr. President, explicitly, generously, candidly: Make no effort to keep Congress in session more than is absolutely necessary and reduce your blacklist to real intentional enemies of the common welfare, you will be astounded to witness the curative effects. . . . You have been a great leader and a great man. You can be again. . . . The chief thing is to eliminate fear and restore confidence—forsake hate and vanity. . . . Permit industry to work alone and in peace. . . . End disturbing scenes, sudden and new proposals to Congress, attacks on groups and individuals who criticize you. . . . You said once with eternal truth that the only thing to fear is fear itself. You should concede the obvious—fear of you.

After that editorial President Roosevelt usually referred to Cissy Patterson as "my dearest friend."

"Have you seen my dearest friend lately?" he asked of Evie Robert on the afternoon of November 18, 1938, over a cocktail at the White House. Evie, the glamorous blonde wife of Assistant Secretary of the Navy "Chip" Robert, was also a *Herald* reporter and an intimate of Cissy Patterson's. "Well," the President continued slyly, "I had a press conference this morning. So don't ask me anything about cherry trees."

Roosevelt was referring to a campaign which Cissy's *Times-Herald* had been promoting throughout the summer and fall of 1938, a campaign to save the cherry trees around Washington's Tidal Basin. The men who wanted to cut down the trees were the members of the commission planning the Jefferson Memorial, headed by the President's uncle, Frederick Delano. The *Times-Herald* conducted a campaign against the memorial, pointing out that Jefferson himself specifically requested that no marble mausoleums be erected in his memory; that if the President's uncle insisted on erecting a monstrosity, he might well avoid the site of the city's most beautiful trees; and that the choice of Frederick Delano as the arbiter of national taste was hardly the result of popular demand. The cherry tree crusade reached its emotional peak when a group of ladies, including *Times-Herald* reporters, chained themselves to the trunks.

"One of the most interesting cases of newspaper flimflam that I have ever seen," pronounced the President in his November 18 morning press conference.

Cissy answered: "It is our campaign, so we accept the slap on the wrist proudly. Though as workers in words, we may shudder at the 'flimflam.' "

While Cissy was fretting over cherry trees, brother Joe was concerned about foreign policy. Patterson couldn't put his finger on it, but he was growing uneasy at Roosevelt's ambiguous reactions to the portentous events in Europe. Patterson hoped that the President would consider the partition of Czechoslovakia arranged in September at Munich a pretty good bargain, considering the Machiavellian nature of the bargainers. Cissy's *Times-Herald,* typically going the *New York News* one better, had cheered the accord: "Thank God for Munich!" The appeasing posture of British Prime Minister Neville Chamberlain at Munich was, said the *Times-Herald,* "almost Christ-like."

But as the fall months rolled by and the winds from

across the Atlantic blew chillier, Roosevelt began to despair of making peace with Hitler. Scanning the daily cables to the White House, he concluded that appeasement was a bad policy, doomed to failure. The President tried not to communicate to the public the extent of his anxiety about the safety of the European democracies. His popularity was at another low point and he felt the public would not sympathize. Since he chose not to identify the crisis, Roosevelt could hardly propose that the United States lend a hand to meet it. Privately, however, the President considered U.S. aid essential. And so the American President quietly daubed medication around the fringes of the European disease. He laid plans for a vastly increased air force, redoubled efforts to aid Jewish refugees to escape Germany, sponsored a hemispheric declaration of joint action against outside threats, and eased restrictions on British and French munitions purchases.

Over the next several years Roosevelt created uneasiness and tension by his delicate attempt to keep apace— and not ahead—of public opinion while he privately formulated his policies on different premises. The President thus exposed himself to bitter attack and charges of "double-dealing" by his political enemies.

Cissy and Joe, with their Midwest Republican backgrounds, were rigidly isolationist. And being Scotch-Irish, they possessed an extra dose of anti-English sentiment. As Joe Patterson explained it in a 1940 editorial, the roots of the family isolationism stretched back to the early nineteenth century, when their ancestors emigrated to America "to get as far away as possible from England." These "Quigleys, Patricks, McCormicks, Pattersons and Medills

harked from Ireland and moved west to the fringes of
civilization, to Chicago"—the ultimate distance from England's political influence.

Far more important was Patterson's experience in
World War I—first as a correspondent, then as a soldier.
His disillusionment with European statecraft and Wil-
sonian idealism was complete; he wrote in his *Notebook
of a Neutral* that "any American in a position of power or
influence who allows any consideration but the selfish
interests of America to guide him is a traitor. . . ."

We must think of America first, Patterson concluded.
"America *über alles.*"

Patterson's thinking in the 1930s was also influenced by
his failure to grasp the remarkable advances in military
technology since his own soldiering days two decades earlier. Though an enthusiastic private pilot, he did not see
the potentialities of the airplane. Patterson could not
conceive how, while the British navy dominated the Atlantic, Hitler constituted a threat to American security.

Patterson did see a threat in the East and he thought
the U.S. ought to do something about it. For years he had
been warning that the expansionist-minded Japanese
would one day covet America's Far East possessions,
and that the United States must expand its Pacific fleet.
"Two ships for one" was the *Daily News* preparedness
slogan, later adopted by the Roosevelt Administration.

Insensitive to the gathering storm in Europe and hy-
persensitive to every tremor in the Orient, Patterson was
ready to misinterpret the President's startling "quarantine
the aggressors" speech. While Patterson had met with the
President only days before the address was delivered in
Chicago, October 5, 1937, he still supposed that Roose-

velt was concerned with Asia and not with Europe. The quarantine concept, so upsetting to the isolationist public, appealed to Patterson as an adaption of his own idea for blockading Japan against further expansion. Colonel McCormick's *Chicago Tribune,* on the other hand, immediately understood the potential implications of the quarantine speech. The *Tribune* commented sourly that Roosevelt's political tutor, Woodrow Wilson, had attempted to keep peace in Europe by the use of economic boycotts and that Roosevelt showed every sign of repeating Wilson's actions. "Mr. Roosevelt repeated his declaration that he hates war," noted the *Tribune.* "He repeated his determination to avoid it. The crowd applauded, . . . the crowd also applauded Mr. Wilson when he campaigned on the slogan, 'He Kept Us Out of War. . . .'"

Soon after the quarantine speech Roosevelt began moves which nobody could misinterpret. In the new session of Congress, FDR mounted a sustained drive to repeal the 1935 Neutrality Act, which severely restricted the material aid America could extend to warring nations. This was tampering with the Magna Carta of isolationism, and it upset Joe and Cissy like nothing he had done before.

In February, 1939, Patterson unburdened himself in a letter to his old friend Lord Beaverbrook, the English newspaper publisher:

> . . . I am not too much given to prayer, but I hope God will let the cup of war pass for a while longer from us.
>
> There is a predominant isolationist sentiment in the United States, I believe, and Roosevelt is acting contrary to the wishes of most of his followers in his present

foreign policy. Of course, in the event of war, our sympathies would get aroused as they did before and we too might be in it. That's what I am afraid of.

By early spring, 1939, the balance in Europe was upset. Hitler seized what was left of Czechoslovakia, Franco marched into Madrid, and Mussolini gobbled up Albania. Chamberlain's government frantically searched for one more exit, and finding none, reluctantly closed the door on peace by guaranteeing the independence of Poland. Within six months that independence disappeared under waves of Nazi troops and the second European war of the twentieth century was on. Shaken, the Congress granted Roosevelt the repeal of the Neutrality Act but attached enough ifs, ands, and buts to remind him he was still "walking on eggs."

Slightly dazed by the cataclysmic developments, Patterson struggled to stay aboard the Roosevelt wagon. Cissy, thinking like a Polish countess, hoped Americans would understand that Hitler would be more merciful than Stalin to Poland, and publicly warned Roosevelt against involvement in Poland's ancient territorial disputes. Like her brother she tried to believe in the President's commitment to neutralism. Following Patterson's lead, she supported Roosevelt for a third term. But during the campaign both brother and sister laced their editorial support with frequent lectures on the evils of interventionism.

In Patterson's *News* the reminders were discreet. In Cissy's *Times-Herald*, the only pro-Roosevelt paper in Washington during the 1940 campaign, they were less so.

12

The Three Furies

No one in the world meant more to Cissy than her
brother Joe, the craggy, loose-tie proletarian. In her later
years, when she left the Hearst nest and assumed full
responsibility as a publisher, she came to rely more upon
Joe than at any time since childhood. But it was Tom
White, not Captain Patterson, who volunteered time and
energy to solve Cissy's publishing problems, Captain Patterson took scant interest in the *Times-Herald*, which he
didn't think a good newspaper. He simply allowed his
sister to imitate his decisions and procedures as best she
could, intervening only if he could prevent her more
embarrassing mistakes. Sister and brother saw each other
infrequently, and often they quarreled.* Cissy was never
quite sure she pleased her brother, and Joe scarcely cared
whether he pleased Cissy or not. Still Cissy idolized him.
He was the family newspaper "genius." He was the foun-
tain of wisdom, the pillar of strength, and the guardian of

* In 1938 Captain Patterson had married Mary King, a newspaperwoman. He commuted to the *News* from Ossining, New York.

righteousness. When Joe was criticized or betrayed or humiliated, so was Cissy. If anything, Cissy felt Joe's misfortunes more deeply than her own. Against her own critics, she lashed out editorially one day and moodily held her peace the next. But in defense of Captain Patterson and his *Daily News* she was a Medea.

Her relationship with her brother explains more than any other factor the bitter and irrational grudge which Cissy formed against the Roosevelt Administration. To be sure, she profoundly differed with the President on the issue of American assistance to the beleaguered European democracies. But she grew to hate FDR for a personal reason—what she considered his unconscionable injustice to her brother. Cissy's break with Roosevelt began a month and a half after his election to a third term and was completed a year later after a searing confrontation between the President and Captain Patterson.

In December, 1940, Roosevelt unveiled his revolutionary Lend-Lease Bill, which permitted the President to lend or lease equipment to nations whose defense he considered essential to American security. Patterson was dumfounded. To him the measure meant the end of neutrality and the probability of American involvement in another European holocaust. He felt personally betrayed by the man he had supported through eight difficult years. While Patterson had sensed the President's shift away from strict neutrality, he had never heard it from Roosevelt.

Shocked and hurt, Patterson wound himself into a knot searching for an explanation. During one long discussion at the Washington home of Senator Shipstead, Patterson burst into tears, crying, "He lied to me, he lied to me."

For most of January, Patterson agonized, fumbling for a way to remain within the Roosevelt camp and simultaneously express editorial opposition to lend-lease. Indecision was an unnatural state for Patterson. He despised Hamlets. He resolved his questioning on January 22 with an editorial denouncing lend-lease and its author:

> Lend-lease gives the President virtual power to take us into war on the side of any country or countries he thinks we should be allied with and to run our entire war effort without consulting Congress as to anything he sees fit to do. Therefore, the bill is a bill to make the President a dictator of the United States, and hence its right name is the "dictatorship bill" instead of the lend-lease bill.

Once having broken with Roosevelt, Patterson forsook moderation. In the blunt, battering-ram style of the *Daily News* editorial page, he inveighed against lend-lease, deprecated the Nazi danger, attacked the alleged U.S. convoying of British ships, and sniped at FDR as a would-be "President of the world." The *News*'s recently strengthened Washington Bureau scoured the capital for damaging signs that the President was preparing for war. One *News* story broke an informal censorship on publicity of U.S. patroling activity and another dispatch brought such a testy administration denial that Patterson's *News* angrily editorialized: "We are afraid the record shows that Mr. Roosevelt has not had an overwhelming respect for truth as truth." Mutual friends, from Patterson's FDR days, appealed to his reason, telling him the President was appalled at being called a liar. Still, there was no retraction.

Only ten months separated Patterson's initial blast at lend-lease and the Japanese attack on Pearl Harbor. Yet that was enough time for the angry publisher to dissipate any gratitude Roosevelt might have felt for Patterson's unswerving support through three election campaigns. Patterson undoubtedly did not appreciate the extent of resentment fostered by his broadside isolationist editorials. When he heard news of the sneak bombing of America's Pacific fleet, Patterson requested an early audience with the President.* Four days after Pearl Harbor he was at the White House. Roosevelt, according to persons who were present, was expecting Patterson to recant the errors of his editorials. Patterson, on the other hand, was coming to offer his services. He had told his family he thought he would be most useful drilling troops in Oklahoma, and he did not expect to keep his rank, in fact, in one emotional moment, he said he would be willing to serve as a sergeant.

Patterson walked into the President's oval office and in his usual blunt manner made his intentions known. For a moment Roosevelt stared at the stocky, unsmiling figure before him. Then, without offering Patterson a seat, he calmly reviewed the *Daily News*'s isolationist campaign, adding that Patterson's misguided passion had delayed the war effort by six months. Grace Tully, Roosevelt's secretary, recalls that FDR said he could not remember an instance in which Patterson's paper had supported a single measure for defense against a potential enemy. Upbraiding the publisher for a lack of patriotism, Roosevelt planted a final arrow in the isolationist's most vulner-

---

* Patterson had received the mistaken information that he would be welcome.

able spot. Many American lives might be lost, he said, because of Patterson's assurance that the U.S. was not in danger.

As the sixty-two-year-old publisher turned to go, tears in his eyes, Roosevelt called out, "One minute, Captain Joe. I want to give you an assignment."

Hardly audible, Patterson replied, "Yes, Mr. President?"

"I want you to go back home and read your editorials for the past six months—read every one and then think over what you have done."

In his long and stormy career Roosevelt treated few people quite so harshly. Perhaps it was a measure of the tension and worry bearing down on the President as he led his country into open war. But it was a serious political blunder. Patterson never forgave nor forgot this impugning of his honor and patriotism. He devoted the rest of his life to avenging the insult, and in the process his own perspective was seriously warped. "All I want to do now is outlive that bastard Roosevelt," Patterson told his family after Pearl Harbor. He did, by thirteen months; but the grim, unreasoning determination behind that macabre wish took most of the joy out of the five years remaining to him. Because of his feud with the President, Joe Patterson, a progressive during his first sixty-two years, is remembered as a reactionary.

For Cissy, Joe's cause became her own. But in her zeal to defend his honor and discredit his detractors, she often went too far—way beyond Joe. Rather pathetically she even elicited his scorn for the embarrassments she printed in his defense. In the public mind Cissy and Joe and Bert, once so different, were accepted throughout the war years as a single voice speaking, in three parts, some of the most virulent and constant criticism of the President and his war aims.

As a new standard for the *Times-Herald* following lend-lease, Cissy like her brother printed a terse message every day on her editorial page. A small conspicuous box reminded readers: "You may fool all of the people some of the time but not all of the people all of the time." In April she wrote to Rose Crabtree in Wyoming: "Some few of us think the President has always intended to get us into war, and that he has led this country as if it was a blindfolded child—little step by little step along the road into the kind of hell this war will surely be."

Cissy allowed no personal friendships to cloud this issue. Lord Beaverbrook, the English newspaper publisher and an intimate friend of Patterson's, was one of her first targets. The press lord presented a set of emeralds to Harry Hopkins' new wife at a wedding reception shortly after the congressional passage of lend-lease. A photograph of the happy occasion was run in the *Tribune* and the *Times-Herald* with the simple caption, "*On receiving lend-lease.*" Another old friend, Bernard Baruch, hosted a party for Hopkins and his bride. Under a *Times-Herald* headline screaming, "NEW DEALER's LAVISH PARTY," Igor Cassini commented that the dinner cost as much as 88,200 bullets. Reprinted in the *Congressional Record*, the article generated hundreds of protest letters.

No one man received more *Times-Herald* invective than Cissy's old soulmate, Harold Ickes, the cantankerous, outspoken Secretary of the Interior. Rarely content with the problems of public lands and Indians, Ickes con-

stantly sought wider fields for the play of his ambitions
and his sharp tongue. In the 1940s, he became one of the
Administration's chief defenders against the isolationist
press. And from the beginning the *Chicago Tribune* was
his prime target. It was a "malevolent" journal, he hissed,
"willing to offend every canon of decency." That was
1939. In short order the *Times-Herald* was coupled with
its Midwest relative in Ickes' denunciations.

Cissy went on radio to retort to Ickes in a speech, mis-
chievously ghosted by Arthur Krock, entitled "The Jaw-
bone of a Ridiculous Man." He, and other New Deal critics of the press, Cissy told the radio audience, were
spreading "poison gas." She concluded: "They fear only
the press as the revealer of their errors and accidents."
During the next four years Cissy's paper hit Ickes high
and low. He was "Harold the bellows," "just a plain bore,"
a guest who "slopped cocktails on other people's rugs," a
politico who used influence to exempt an aide from the
draft. Cissy threw herself into the task of deflating Ickes,
scribbling notes to her reporters to check out this or that
lead. And when there was nothing better, the *Times-
Herald* "exposed" Ickes' use of a government truck in his
private egg business.

A gamecock by nature, Ickes returned scratch for
scratch. Cissy and her cousin Bert were sure that malice
prompted his official opposition to a *Tribune*-sponsored
lakefront airport for Chicago, and his initiation of an air
force base near Cissy's Dower House in Maryland.

The *Times-Herald* routinely pelted the more liberal
members of the Roosevelt Administration with rotten
eggs. Henry Wallace's foreign policy musings earned him
the epithet "crystal ball gazing crackpot." Harry Hopkins

was summarily dismissed as "the Iowa boy who never earned a cent in his life." Hopkins, a nervous, chain-smoking ex-social worker, wrecked his health in the serv-ice of Roosevelt. In 1944, when Hopkins was in the hospi-tal, FDR wrote him an affectionate admonishment to stay away from Washington until his health returned. "If you come back before the end of June," the President wrote, "you will be extremely unpopular with everybody with the exception of Cissy Patterson who wants to kill you off as soon as possible—just as she does me."

Cissy's journalistic sorties ranged all over the capital from as high as Supreme Court Justice Felix Frankfurter to Attorney General Francis Biddle and on down to col-umnist Drew Pearson. Frankfurter was compared to the cunning and unscrupulous seventeenth-century French statesman, Cardinal Richelieu, who so strengthened the French throne that a revolution was eventually needed to redistribute power to the people. The *Times-Herald* in-vited readers to draw the same conclusion about Frank-furter's brand of brain trusting. Large photographs, side by side, drew attention to an alleged similarity in the crafty eyes of the Frenchman and the New Dealer. Drew Pearson, no longer an employee or a substitute son after lend-lease, became in the *Times-Herald* a twentieth-century Robespierre, who liked children and flowers and the taste of human blood.

Such Sunday feature treatment was the epitome of *Times-Herald* invective and the paper lavished prepara-tion and imagination on its vendettas. A striking two-page layout on March 14, 1943, zeroed in on Biddle and two other Washington-based members of the prestigious Phil-adelphia family. Accompanied by unflattering photographs, the article ridiculed Francis Biddle's youthful poetry, Ambassador Anthony Biddle's dapper clothes, and painter George Biddle's penchant for drawing family portraits in murals for the Justice Department.

Behind the diatribe was a series of irritations—some major and some minor—inflicted on Cissy by Biddle's Justice Department. Federal officers working for Justice had investigated two of Cissy's foreign employees for possible espionage; and one new member of the *Times-Herald* staff turned out to be an informer who worked simultaneously for the Justice Department, the Department of the Interior, and for Drew Pearson. But Cissy considered Biddle a nemesis chiefly for the part he played in two controversial episodes of 1942—Marshall Field III's attempt to break the Associated Press monopoly and the government's attempt to prosecute the *Tribune* for violating wartime censorship in its coverage of the battle of Midway.

Field, a recent convert to liberalism, had founded the *Chicago Sun* in December, 1941, for the specific purpose of breaking the *Tribune*'s morning monopoly and providing a pro-Roosevelt voice in the urban center of America's Midwest. To compete against such a well-equipped and wealthy newspaper as the *Tribune*, Field needed the solid base of Associated Press world-wide coverage. But the *Tribune* held the rights to AP service in Chicago and would not consider making it available to a competitor.

Just how much interest the Roosevelt Administration took in Field's venture became obvious at the 1942 AP meeting. Archibald MacLeish, speaking for the administration, clearly intimated that the government felt that the AP was a monopoly which ought to put its house in order before federal action was necessary. Outside the hall agents from Biddle's Justice Department were conspicuously evident.

To Cissy the government's intervention on behalf of Field was doubly galling. Not only was he in direct competition with a McCormick-Patterson paper, but he was receiving the very government assistance which Cissy had once asked for and been denied. Since 1937, when her paper was still friendly to Roosevelt, Cissy had been attempting to obtain AP service, but her application had been blackballed by the two Washington papers with Associated Press membership, the *Post* and the *Star*. Before the war she had asked her friend, Assistant Attorney General Thurmond Arnold, why he did not initiate anti-trust proceedings against the AP. Arnold had demurred from starting a government suit but had indicated that he would prosecute one if Cissy lighted fires under the issue. Editorial support for Roosevelt's third-term bid would not harm her cause, Arnold implied.

Incensed, Cissy refused to barter with the Justice Department. As she recounted the meeting with Arnold at the 1942 AP session, "I come from four generations of newspaper people and I didn't like it. I didn't like the smell of it."

The AP directors were angry at what they considered administration prying into their affairs, and after the 1942 meeting they slapped a suspension on all membership applications. Biddle's Justice Department, however, proceeded with its action and eventually broke the AP monopoly.

Cissy fired on everyone who had a hand in the controversy—from Marshall Field to his New York editor of

PM, Ralph Ingersoll, to Biddle, to Archibald MacLeish, lampooning the latter's poetry as well as his appearance at the AP meeting as a government spokesman. Roosevelt later wrote MacLeish welcoming him to the "society of immortals," those excoriated by the *Chicago Tribune* family. "The trouble is," Roosevelt wrote, "that Bertie, Joe Patterson and Cissy deserve neither hate nor praise, only pity for their unbalanced mentalities."

Attorney General Biddle was also a principal figure in the administration's attack on the *Tribune* for publishing (and the *Times-Herald* for republishing) a detailed account of the June naval battle off Midway Island. The Office of War Information and other censorship authorities charged the *Tribune* with giving away to the Japanese the crucial information that United States cryptographers had broken Japanese codes and ciphers. Attorney General Biddle held a grand jury investigation in Chicago, but during the middle of it the Navy Department enigmatically declined to reveal further information about the incident. There never was an official explanation from the Navy Department for why it short-circuited the government's case. However, after the war, Adlai Stevenson told a naval historian that the case had been dropped because the *Tribune* story had been passed by a Navy censor. Biddle, as he said himself, felt like a fool.

Cissy never had intended to undermine the morale of the nation while it was at war, but her injudicious editorial decisions opened her to just such a charge. She had, of course, opposed entrance into the war, and she entertained no affection for those directing the war effort, nor for their conceptions of a postwar world. But the morning after Pearl Harbor she reprinted her brother's editorial: "Well, we're in it. God knows Americans didn't want it. But let's get behind our President and fight for America first."

Cissy did stay behind the President but instead of heeling, she too often nipped at his ankles. The Midway incident was only the most memorable of a number of Cissy's scrapes. Her first major clash with the administration came only four days before Pearl Harbor. Cissy reprinted the *Chicago Tribune*'s account of a United States contingency war plan. The story, written by the *Tribune*'s Chesly Manley, revealed the "Rainbow Five Plan" for potential U.S. troop commitment to Europe and North Africa. The document, which was as thick as a book, had been relayed to the *Tribune* by Senator Burton K. Wheeler, the Montana isolationist, who had been given his copy by sympathetic Air Force officers.

Without hesitation McCormick reprinted portions of the explosive document, crowing that it was the "best scoop in the history of journalism." On the other hand, an editor at Patterson's *Daily News* decided not to reprint the plan, and the *News* simply ran a story about the *Tribune* scoop and its implications. Patterson later said that was what his editors were paid for—to have sense. In Washington the *Times-Herald* ran the original *Tribune* disclosure under a banner headline. The next morning copies of the *Tribune* and the *Times-Herald* were passed from hand to hand among disturbed congressmen. Roosevelt grimly declined to comment at a regular news conference. But later in the day Secretary of War Henry Stimson read a prepared statement, denouncing those responsible for the leak as unpatriotic and disloyal. At a subsequent Cabinet meeting there was talk of prosecuting Colonel McCormick for violation of the Espionage Act or for conspiracy, but the suggestion was dismissed because "Rainbow Five" had been written as a peacetime prospectus and not as an operational war plan.

Cissy hadn't needed to reprint *Tribune-News* material to get in trouble with the administration. She was quite capable of ruffling bureaucratic feathers with her own carping. A prime example of Cissy as an independent irritant was a 1944 editorial which attacked the State Department for harboring socially prominent young officers whom she felt ought to be on the front lines. What had roused Cissy's ire was a Roosevelt announcement that pre-medical students under twenty-six years of age no longer would receive draft deferments. In a signed editorial, entitled "Some State Department Boys Who Do Not Choose to Fight," Cissy ridiculed twenty young State Department officers as a "panty waist brigade" who sat behind desks while potential doctors risked their lives.

"This company of pretties," she caustically suggested, were performing jobs that just as well could be handled by young women, "who may or may not prove as decorative in the better drawing rooms of Washington." Photographs of the twenty offenders were lined up on the *Times-Herald* page like a police line-up. As happened on several occasions, a Cabinet officer stepped forward to berate Cissy. This time it was Cissy's frequent party guest, Secretary of State Cordell Hull, the dignified, crusty Tennessee gentleman. He convened a press conference to denounce Cissy's charges as "violent" and "unfair." For the record Hull detailed the draft and marriage status of his junior officers, all but four of whom were serving overseas. No one under twenty-six had been deferred.

Cissy replied with a second editorial, "Them Was Weasel Words, Mr. Hull," lambasting the secretary for failing to note that none of the twenty young men were in fighting service. Furthermore, Cissy disputed Hull's statistics showing a highly favorable ratio of State personnel at distant battlefronts. She charged Hull with including State's overseas janitorial, maintenance, and secretarial staffs in his calculations. Too many able-bodied men remained at State in Washington doing nonessential work, she insisted. This time, Hull was silent. At the *Times-Herald* a memo to the city desk followed: "Mrs. Patterson thinks this should be kept alive."

Cissy's editorial judgment was never more questionable than on the tragic plight of European Jewry. She was horrified at the German atrocities, but before the full extent of the genocide was incontrovertably known, Cissy intimated broadly that the horror accounts were being overplayed by Jewish executives within the communications industry (just as she claimed British agents had distorted German conduct in Belgium during World War I). Cissy contended during the early war period that Europe could survive fascism but not communism. She reprinted questionable articles from the *New York Daily News;* the most notorious was John O'Donnell's account of General George S. Patton, Jr., slapping a panicked Jewish soldier, which seemed to imply that Jewishness had a connection with cowardice.

Jewish businessmen withdrew a substantial amount of advertising, despite reminders from the *Times-Herald* business office that Cissy's second husband had been, after all, a Jew. Ugly letters flooded the *Times-Herald* suggesting that Cissy was a traitor—one compared her to Eva Braun, another ranted that her newspaper wasn't fit to line garbage cans. Such letters from readers stung Cissy. She filed them among her personal records.

In New York an organization called Freedom House attempted to publish a full-page advertisement in *The New York Times* with pictures of Cissy, Patterson, and McCormick under a headline, "CAN THEY BE TREA-SONOUS?" which publisher Arthur Sulzberger declined to print. But anti-American charges began to fly faster and thicker. *Life* Magazine labeled the *Tribune* and the *Times-Herald* the Bibles of pro-Nazi and defeatist groups throughout the country. In Congress freshman Pennsylvania Democrat Elmer Holland launched an attack on Patterson, McCormick, and Cissy for "hating Roosevelt more than they hate Hitler." Exercising congressional immunity from libel, Holland claimed "Patterson and his little sister Cissy are more dangerous by far than the half-cracked tools of Goebbels. . . ."

"You're a liar, Congressman Holland," Patterson replied editorially, and Cissy reprinted the editorial, adding her own signed postscript: "You're a liar, and you know it."

"How dare they!" was Cissy's reaction to the charges of disloyalty which flew at her from all directions. She had publicly pledged her support to American victory and, though the public had no way of knowing it, had backed up that pledge in a significant letter to a Polish aristocrat. In the difficult days at the time of Pearl Harbor the Polish official had tested her sympathies in the hopes they weren't anti-German. In reply she had written, "All the world sufficiently interested to listen knows that I haven't approved this administration's foreign policy. But all of that is over the dam now. *Now* we Americans have to stand and we will stand together, 100 per cent."

"We could not understand," Cissy told a District of Columbia judge, "why the Winchells, the Pearsons, the Ingersolls, the Backers [of the *New York Post*] kept screaming and yelling at us—about what? Who are they indeed to question the loyalty of such Americans as I and my brother?" Cissy's question was asked during a libel suit she filed against Columnist Walter Winchell for broadcasting that her editorials were read and approved by Nazi agents. Though Cissy dropped the libel suit for an out-of-court settlement, she singed Winchell's ears with a *Times-Herald* scorcher headlined in 64-point type, "COCKROACH!" The article roundly lambasted Winchell as "a potential feelthy picture king" for his peephole journalism. "He is forever boasting that he is the American Hitler would most like to hang. In what respect does that make Hitler different from anybody else?" Cissy's newspaper, which once had carried Winchell's column, asked.

During the libel proceedings Winchell's lawyers tried to prove that Cissy was chronically vindictive. They asked if it wasn't true that when Columnist Drew Pearson narrowly missed death in a plane crash, she had called the escape "a matter of regret."

Cissy fought the most protracted and saddest of her wartime feuds with Drew Pearson. Cissy celebrated her sixtieth birthday with the Pearson family, November 7, 1941, and that was the last happy occasion they spent together.

The unveiling of lend-lease had forced everyone to show his cards, and Pearson's were decidedly pro-Roosevelt. Cissy instructed that the column, co-authored by Pearson and Robert Allen, be edited into line with *Times-Herald* editorials. Shortly after Pearl Harbor, Pearson asked to be released. He objected to the continual cutting and to placement on the comics page.

On February 7 Cissy replied, "You are perfectly right, dear Drew, both from your point of view and my own. Long disgusted with your column, I decided to cancel it out shortly after December 7." For the next several months the two conducted a bitter public row over the issue of whether Pearson and Allen had quit or been fired. Cissy published front-page explanations which accused them of "poisonous attempts to smear the reputation of a great soldier and in our opinion one of the greatest Americans of all time, General Douglas MacArthur."

The columnists countered with a full-page advertisement. When the other Washington newspapers declined to print it, the columnists settled for a news story explaining their side of the controversy. They quit, Pearson and Allen said, over a fundamental issue: "We did not believe President Roosevelt was pushing this nation into war."

Pearson and Allen offered their services to Eugene Meyer's *Post*. Meyer was not at all anxious to intervene in one of Cissy's family quarrels, but a circulation-builder like the "Washington Merry-Go-Round" column was hard to turn down. Pearson and Allen were hired on the unusual terms, that they consent to having their column appear in the second section, in back of the comics—just where Cissy had relegated them.

Throughout the war and afterward Cissy kept up a running commentary on Pearson and he reciprocated fact for fact, rumor for rumor, innuendo for innuendo. "The craziest woman in Washington should be out any edition," he told a radio audience in 1942. The fine Italian intrigues which the two wove behind the presses and microphones would amaze anyone unfamiliar with detectives, miniature cameras, telephone devices, and other sneaky machines.

As the war drew to a close in Europe, Cissy endured the final disillusionment of seeing Poland submerged under a blanket of Russian troops. Since 1938, when the *Times-Herald* had run a series warning of the double-edged sword hanging over Poland and the other East European nations, Cissy had been warning against just such an end. She had persistently repeated that Stalin intended to claim Poland as war booty, and she had never budged from her belief that it would be a worse fate than German occupation.

"Excepting for the Jewish population," she had observed in a 1939 radio talk, "my guess is that today any Pole would prefer to live under German rule than Russian rule."

Cissy, of course, knew and loved only one Poland, that of the landed aristocrats. She conceded that the Nazis would loot the wealth and the land. But she thought the Communists presented a more pernicious threat, because they would liquidate her blue-blooded friends. Throughout the war Cissy attempted in the *Times-Herald* to keep the Polish predicament in the public consciousness. After all, the fate of Poland had been the issue which officially started the war. And the probability that Poland would come under Russian hegemony agonized Cissy. She lashed out bitterly at Roosevelt "for not saying anything" while the Russian army paused to allow the Germans to put down the eleventh-hour Warsaw uprising. The Yalta agreement, insuring the free movement of Soviet troops through East Europe to Berlin, deepened her gloom.

"Poland is the litmus paper by which to test the acidity in the milk of post-war planning," the *Times-Herald* had stated. Now, even before war's end, she was ready to pass judgment. In early 1945 the *Times-Herald* editorialized: "FDR gambled in war, the sport of kings—staked by the American people—and went bust."

In a last burst of vindictiveness Cissy printed a page of pictures in early 1945 that showed nothing but dead and mangled bodies of U.S. soldiers. One photograph showed a GI corpse on a beach; another a bloody, wounded soldier on a stretcher; a third a figure badly mangled by a bomb, and so on. In the middle of the page in a box Roosevelt's 1940 campaign pledge was quoted: "And while I am talking to you mothers and fathers, I give you one more assurance. I say it again and again and again, your boys are not going to be sent into any foreign wars."

Roosevelt was soon immune from such attacks. The President, whom Cissy had once praised for winning ways and then maligned for Caesarism, collapsed from a massive cerebral hemorrhage and died on April 12, 1945.

Cissy tried to respect Roosevelt in death as she had not in life. She ordered her editors to clear the front page for a black-bordered picture of the dead Chief Executive that would be fittingly dignified. But her orders were misunderstood—perhaps the staff was too used to picking at the man—and the first edition of the *Times-Herald* front page looked tacky. With resignation she wrote to an editor, "Maybe next time a President dies in office, *maybe* we will know better what to do."

13

Gall and Wormwood

In June, 1943, during a withering heat spell, Cissy collapsed unconscious at Dupont Circle. Her servants, panicking when she did not revive, searched for assistance in Cissy's personal telephone book, which contained a bewildering list of lawyers, veterinarians, caterers, clubs, body masseurs, ten animal hospitals, alcoholics anonymous, twelve hospitals, five nurses, and twenty-two doctors.

From the array of possibilities, the servants picked the name of Dr. Eugene de Savitch, probably because they remembered him as a suavely handsome extra man at Cissy's dinner parties. Savitch was a Russian émigré, whose slick bedside manner had helped him build a large Society practice. He had first won Cissy's gratitude in 1940 by driving to Dower House to treat a bad case of poison ivy. After that he became such a favorite that Cissy invited him on trips and to parties in Florida as well as in Washington. No doubt he reminded her of the times when she was courted and flattered in Poland by other European men.

Cissy herself would not have called on Savitch for anything more serious than aches and pains. But she was in no condition to protest when he scurried to Dupont Circle and took complete charge of the case. When she revived, Cissy found herself in an oxygen tent closeted alone in a second-floor suite. Outside her door Savitch was selecting which of her friends might visit her and periodically issuing forecasts of death.

"I do not think you will see Mrs. Patterson again," he told a *Times-Herald* executive. "She has suffered a massive heart attack. You will have to run the newspaper on your own."

Telephone calls, inquiring memos, and newspapers were forbidden by Savitch, who insisted that his patient must not be upset. But doctor's orders or no doctor's orders, William Shelton, Cissy's business manager, continued to send each day's editions to Dupont Circle. "Otherwise, we'll catch hell when she comes out," he tersely observed.

Though weakened by her collapse and drowsy with drugs, Cissy was conscious enough to worry about Savitch's diagnosis. "I don't know whether I believe him or not," she wrote to Rose Crabtree ten days after her collapse. "Maybe if I didn't live in this outrageous house with cupids stringing marble wreaths all over the god damned place, he wouldn't try to keep me as an invalid . . . anyhow, I feel perfectly well now."

Savitch continued to bar friends from the sickroom and adamantly refused every suggestion of calling in any but his personal choice of a consulting physician.

"Evie," Cissy finally wrote Mrs. Roberts, "Please come see me. I'm sick, I don't know what's happened." When

Savitch discovered Evie in Cissy's room, he reddened and exploded in frenzy. "You, you get out of here! I left orders that nobody was to disturb my patient." But Evie had had time to sample the food on Cissy's breakfast tray and she said it had nauseated her. Cissy, hypersuspicious by nature, felt her worst fears confirmed—Savitch was trying to drug her, she concluded, in an attempt to influence her will.

Through her secretary Cissy summoned editor Frank Waldrop. Physically pushing his way past the protesting doctor, Waldrop found Cissy weak and pale and terrified. Waving him close, she whispered, "Get me a doctor, this man is trying to kill me." Waldrop obtained the consulting doctor of Cissy's choice. Electrocardiagrams were taken and a firm diagnosis made. Cissy had suffered no heart attack.

A year later Dr. Paul Dudley White, the renowned heart specialist, reviewed the case and also concluded that Cissy had "a nice little heart." White attributed her collapse to a high-strung nervous system. Indeed, White noted, the attack was only the latest and worst of several nervous prostrations Cissy had suffered, the first dating back to 1900, when she was forced to leave Miss Porter's School.

Although Savitch was unmasked as an incompetent at best, he conserved enough cheek to present Cissy with a bill for $10,000. That was the *coup de grâce* which kept Cissy in a mild state of fury throughout the five months she spent recuperating in Florida and Long Island. By December, Cissy was back at the *Times-Herald,* and during an elevator conversation she told Shelton she was "still on the rampage against Savitch and his Luminal" drug. She said he ought to be exposed in the paper as a quack. The remark was passed on to the editorial department, and within three weeks *Times-Herald* reporters had amassed material from all over the country for a front-page exposé. One part-time reporter quit the project, complaining to Cissy, "What you want is not a reporting job but a typical Patterson-Hearst character assassination." The Savitch story did bear too many marks of a personal vendetta and *Times-Herald* readers complained. So did the doctor, who sued for libel. He lost the case but after filing an appeal the *Times-Herald* decided to end the affair with a modest out-of-court settlement. For Savitch it was a meager triumph. Hs reputation was ruined and he was forced to leave Washington.

Cissy was greatly unnerved by the experience. She had worried about declining health, but now she was obsessed by it. For once Cissy attempted to follow doctor's advice. She reduced her smoking and switched to filtered cigarettes, and she experimented with turtle soup laced with sherry in place of whiskey by the tumbler. She attempted to get enough rest, taking frequent trips, and she tackled insomnia, instructing her servants to maintain utter silence while she was attempting to sleep. At Dower House the gardeners were ordered to refrain from mowing the lawn until the mistress of the house was up and about. Her rooms were sprayed with floral mist to banish imagined odors and her bed linen was changed several times a day to guard against dirt and germs.

But no illness preoccupied Cissy or filled her with such speechless horror as the thought that she might become insane or senile. "Mind and memory quite gone," she had written twenty years earlier about her mother, whose mental and physical decline had sickened Cissy at the time. Now senility was her private nightmare. She wrote a letter, which she had notarized, and sent several copies to intimate friends, requesting that none of her family be allowed to see her if she lost control of her faculties. She asked a *Times-Herald* editor to research what treatment the Air Force was giving pilots with psychosomatic illnesses. And she interviewed a psychiatrist about the effect of protein and nicotine on the brain.

Cissy's mental reactions were not as sharp as they once were. Absent-mindedness plagued her. She couldn't hold on to anything. Her staff stashed pencils, cigarette holders, handkerchiefs, and glasses in every room so that a servant could replace a lost item almost as soon as Madam buzzed for it. Often she pushed her eyeglasses up on her head and swore they had disappeared—she couldn't see anymore without them—but rather than point out the obvious, the servants would hand her a second pair.

Always impulsive, Cissy's behavior now became impossibly erratic. She was capable of ordering terrapin, filet mignon, and cherries jubilee for a dinner of eight at Dower House only to change her mind at the last moment and decide to have twelve for dinner in town. One chef turned in his hat when he realized he had carted a single wild duck back and forth five times between Washington and Maryland.

With friends she gyrated wildly from one extreme to the other. She indulged in fits of thoughtful generosity. But without warning and often without reason Cissy would break into insults and denunciations. "Lots of times I'd be preparing a big dinner," her cook remembers, "and the butler would come down and say that Mrs. Patterson got in a fight with the guests and they'd all gone home."

Cissy went to parties prepared to leave. "I don't think I'll stay through dinner," she would warn her chauffeur upon arrival. "I can't stand this crowd." Sure enough, within half an hour Cissy would sail back out to her car.

"I can't keep friends longer than six months," she admitted.

The anxious indecision of her private life was carried over into her professional life. She felt a terrible lassitude after the Savitch experience and a wish to quit, and on the other hand a terrible fear of making any commitments which would indicate withdrawal.

She would tell her editors to run the paper and the very next day start scheming to get back full control. At times, realizing how difficult she made the day-to-day operation of the paper, she would apologize. "Don't you see," she would say on such occasions, "it's *all* I have left. If I let you alone, what am I to do?"

Cissy's contributions in the *Times-Herald* became embarrassingly apparent. Her editorials and articles warned against the dangers of drugs, the evils of drunkenness, the horrors of mental illness. In an editorial entitled "Sick, Sick, Sick" she lashed out at physical and emotional perverts. She expressed her revulsion at women who drank too much in another editorial, "Drunken Dames." Her special condemnation for personal and political enemies was to imply that they saw psychiatrists. In one article, that outspat all others, she placed her New Deal *bêtes noires* in an insane asylum, describing minutely their aberrations.

The loneliness and insecurity which produced such attacks were also apparent in the *Times-Herald*. While writing of a public issue, she would inadvertently dwell on herself, such as in a 1946 attack on the prosecution of Germans who had looted jewelry and art from other countries during the war. "We can imagine how few voices would be raised," she wrote, "if the knicknacks of an old lady in this town, in this office to be exact, were liberated in the same fashion."

To the public Cissy had always seemed arrogant, self-assured, and oblivious to criticism in a Marie Antoinette fashion. She was the *grande dame*, who could paddle down her swimming pool in Palm Beach—sunglasses astride nose and straw hat atop head, spreading a thin film of sun lotion across the surface of the water, pursued by a hairy poodle. She was the spendthrift, who on the spur of the moment would take her private railroad car to Williamsburg—stopping only long enough to observe "how quaint" from the station platform before returning. She was the mistress of power, who acted on the assumption that rules could be changed to fit her needs. Tickets to the premiere of *Gone With the Wind* had been sold out for six months, but when Cissy decided at the last minute to attend, it was arranged—with a chartered plane for the flight to Atlanta and a police escort through town to the movie theater.

But those close to her were more aware of the terrible toll the tensions and hatreds of the war years had exacted from Cissy's self-confidence and self-esteem.

Time magazine labeled her "the most hated woman in

America," and Cissy was inclined to agree at times. Though she presented a plucky front, Cissy was mortified at being so roundly disliked. It confirmed her feeling that without money she would never have gotten anywhere. The other side of such self-pity was suspicion—of friends, of the wide world, and most consistently of people who worked for her. She was continually firing servants she thought were cheating her. When the huge monthly bills for her household came in, she would berate C. B. Porter, her nervous and fastidious financial advisor. She commanded him to find the offenders, ignoring his protests that her own odd hours, expensive tastes, and unannounced parties accounted for most of the waste.

Periodically Cissy prowled through Dupont Circle on her own time-and-motion studies. "You couldn't hear her sneaking up behind you," recalled a housemaid. "She made no noise. You had to be careful." Once on a surprise visit in the middle of the day to Dower House, she found one of her chauffeurs standing in the middle of the driveway, rag in hand, panting with exhaustion. "What's wrong," she inquired. He had been working hard was the reply. "You're a damn liar," she said sourly, and as often happened, she was right. Her servants called her psychic.

Cissy's sense of persecution sparked deeper suspicions. Who was it that wanted to kill her? She wasn't sure but with all the hate around there must be someone with such dark motives. Whoever it was planted the rattlesnake in her tissue box at Dower House. She found the snake with a scream while powdering her face and gossiping with Evie Roberts one day in the dressing room. Rattlers were common in Maryland and needed no assistance to get where this one was found, coiled among the tissues, but to Cissy it was a plot, and to guard against such plots, she kept guns—one in her purse, one in the limousine, and another by her bedside. In a Dower House closet was a box of Colt pistols in case replacements were needed.

And as if to add excitement and possible meaning to her disordered life, Cissy began intimating to friends that when she died, they should look for signs of foul play.

In such a hostile world Cissy's lifelong love of animals became a dependency. Her daughter explained that one reason her mother loved animals so extravagantly was that they were uncritically loyal and didn't talk back. Cissy stocked Dower House as if it was a zoo, and her most constant companions were a bevy of poodles. Although Cissy was an experienced animal trainer, she indulged her last poodles to the point where they became offensively neurotic. They were given the run of the house and made messes everywhere which the servants were supposed to clean up. Butch, a favorite poodle, tore furniture, strewed toilet paper up and down the staircase, and lunged at the chauffeur whenever he opened the limousine door. When a poodle named Toto swallowed a stone, Cissy called in an eminent surgeon and bought an operating table, lights, and surgical equipment for the crisis. Toto convalesced in a baby crib, where he was fed cracked ice and snippets of quail in a silver spoon held by his mistress.

It was not just desperate affection which accounted for such an incident, but also a morbid fear of dying. Her own health declining, Cissy dwelt on death, and all she could see before her was an angry Calvinist God consigning her to damnation. For relief Cissy turned to Roman Catholicism, the faith which offered remission of sins to repenters. She took instructions from Father Edmund Walsh of Georgetown University and she spoke frequently of the faith with Msgr. Fulton J. Sheen, whose radio addresses enthralled her.

For a while Cissy drew comfort from a simple Polish priest who had come to Dupont Circle to perform last rites for her maid, Kashka. She saw him several times and he composed a prayer for her: "My God, I doubt your presence and even existence. I wish to be happy as I was being a child. Nobody really and truly loves me. Help me."

A light note was added to Cissy's experimentation with Catholicism by her zany friend and co-experimenter Evalyn Walsh McLean. Speaking in the material language they both knew best, Cissy gave Evalyn a large diamond crucifix as a memento of their search for faith. To please Cissy, Evalyn appeared one night at a party in Dupont Circle wearing the crucifix around her neck.

"My God, Evalyn!" Cissy gasped. "I meant for you to hang that thing over your bed."

"Well, my God, Cissy," came the reply, "I couldn't bring my bed could I?"

At the end of her life Cissy's closest friends were nearly all Catholics. Brother Joe had converted in 1938. Tom White, her most intimate friend, was a lifelong Catholic, as were Evie Roberts and Anne Bowie Smith.

But though Cissy asked for a Catholic burial, she never became a convert. Her roots in a stern Calvinism were too strong. She wanted consolation and salvation through Catholicism, but she could not rid herself of prejudices inculcated in her childhood that the Church of Rome was corrupt and voluptuous—an indulgence like psychiatry.

Holidays were especially cruel to Cissy. They heightened her loneliness and doubt. To dispel the ghosts of Christmas she gave annual parties at Dupont Circle, with champagne and live ponies and presents for everyone, but it was "not a favorite time." Neither was November 7, her birthday. Drew Pearson feted her every year from 1929 to 1941, and from then, until she died, Mrs. McLean assumed the responsibility. In 1947, with no one left to treat her, Cissy put up the money for several young friends to throw her a "surprise" birthday party at Dupont Circle. She missed the old friends. "You know darling," she wrote Rose Crabtree, "years may come and years may go, but you know how I have always loved you and I think it is kind of mean of you not to make a little effort."

Newer acquaintances wondered why Cissy kept around a grouchy old character like Cal Carrington. Cal was an aging, mangy fixture at Cissy's country houses, who snarled at servants and guests indiscriminantly, and it was clear that his presence unnerved his hostess. "I wish he wouldn't put his boots up on the furniture," she would say. "I wish he'd stop clacking his false teeth." Yet Cissy indulged the old wolf as she indulged her poodles. He was an ancient friend, and loyal. She hadn't any to spare, for the inner circle of friends and relations she had long relied upon was disintegrating.

She was split irrevocably from her daughter, who could not respond to her mother's increasingly desperate gestures of affection. A lifetime of wrongs, on both sides, stood between them. Cissy had tried to react gallantly to Felicia's stormy resentments for her neglected youth. When her daughter wrote two novels, *House of Violence* and *Flower and Smoke,* attacking her mother and the family, Cissy quietly took her punishment. "Now that you've written two books on the subject, hadn't you better try something else?" she suggested.

But when she was alone, Cissy's fury burst forth at being so coldly rejected. One night, Adela St. John remembers, Cissy stood on the landing at Dupont Circle hurling crockery at Felicia's portrait, screaming, "You're a terrible girl." When asked the next morning why she did it, Cissy broke into tears. Friends of both parties tried unsuccessfully to reconcile the rift. Joe Patterson tried, and so did Cal Carrington and Evalyn McLean. Shortly before she died Cissy asked Felicia to meet her for dinner in New York, but Felicia panicked and didn't appear. At their next meeting Cissy lost her temper and Felicia walked out for the last time, saying, "I won't be a witness to this violence."

For a time Cissy transferred her starving affections to her red-headed granddaughter, Ellen, the issue of Felicia's marriage to Drew Pearson. She contributed lavishly to Ellen's support, giving her property, furniture, jewelry, and paying the salary of her governess. Ellen, and Drew and his second wife were the closest thing to a family for Cissy. But she had been warned by brother Joe that it was a sand family which would wash away in the first storm. The storm came when Pearson's columns began attacking Cissy's isolationist relatives and friends. Maddened by what she considered betrayal, Cissy stomped and kicked until her sand family was a hole in the beach. Ellen, dismayed by the public name-calling, said she did not want to see her grandmother again. When she married Thurmond Arnold's son, in 1946, Cissy refused the invitation to her wedding.

Substitutes took the place of substitutes in Cissy's life. Her last ladies-in-waiting were Evie Roberts and Anne Smith, who were lovely-looking and gay and who visited her when she was sick. And she had Frank Waldrop as an equerry. But she had no family life. Her brother Joe did not find out about her 1943 attack until days later, which was an illustration of how separate their lives were, despite Cissy's strong emotional attachment to her brother. In the later years Captain Patterson was always slightly embarrassed and angered by Cissy. And after his humiliation by Roosevelt, Captain Joe was too involved in his own problems to extend much consolation to his sister.

Cissy's method of expressing her attachment was in part responsible for Joe's wish to remain at a distance. Jealous of others close to him, she once offered a toast at dinner, proposing the death of his second wife. She told stories about him, some false, hoping to impress people that she knew more about Joe than anyone else. A 1938 *New Yorker* profile told of how Captain Joe as a little boy had strangled a canary in a rage. Cissy never admitted inventing the tale, but she was the culprit in her brother's eyes.

Cissy was constantly inviting her brother for weekends at Dower House and he was continually offering excuses. But when he unexpectedly agreed once to visit, Cissy remarked wistfully to a friend, "I'll have to invite some other people. You know, I bore Joe so terribly." If there was a replacement in Cissy's heart for Joe, it was Tom White, the charming, virile Irishman she fell in love with after she was fifty. As Hearst's general manager he had held her hand and pulled her through the crisis of becoming a newspaper publisher, advising, cajoling, lending time and expertise. But grateful though Cissy was the relationship could not fill the void: White was married.

In time the passion burned out, but unlike so many of her other relationships, Cissy and White remained the closest of friends until they died—within a month of each other in 1948. It was the last romantic affair of Cissy's life and when it was transformed into friendship, Cissy suddenly seemed to age. For some fifteen years she had struggled against the clock, submitting to masseurs and facial experts and scalp invigorators, and tinting her hair with henna.

But Cissy's charms met enemies more formidable than mere time. Loneliness and anxiety and tension and fatigue, drinking and smoking and late hours, were what grayed her porcelain skin, thickened her willow waist, and cut ugly lines under her fierce brown eyes. She lost her interest in clothes and gave hundreds of dresses away. She carelessly restocked by ordering favorite items in gross lots from Bergdorf Goodman—thirty pairs of the same shoes, ten of the same bathing suit. But she preferred to wear the same dress over and over, until her maid would cry, "Please, Mrs. Patterson, not *that* again!" In her house she wore slacks and flat-heeled shoes.

Cissy's longtime friends charitably remembered her graceful characteristics, even in her decline. "She was a leopard not a lion," specified Evie Roberts. "She didn't move pad after pad, but in a continuous liquid motion." To Adela Rogers St. John, Cissy was Queen Elizabeth incarnate, sitting in front of a roaring fire at Dower House, dressed in a green velvet teagown trimmed with sable, holding in her lap two cats the color of her hair. Arthur Krock cherished an image of Cissy sitting on a sofa, little pink feet curled beneath her, telling stories in a soft low lyrical voice about the days of her childhood . . . "and then Aunt Kate locked Bertie in the closet. . . ."

But to people who met her late in life, the glamour was invisible under the silt of time. "I can't see how anybody could have said she was attractive," recalled a man who started work on the *Times-Herald* when Cissy was in her sixties. "I thought she was downright ugly, with that gravel voice, and that scowl and the pants she wore."

To the general public Cissy became one of the sights of Washington as she took her daily constitutional along the expressway beside the Potomac River. It was a bizarre parade: a pack of big rowdy poodles in front and a chauffeured Cadillac following sedately behind. Cissy, though she looked like Halloween in her dog-walking "disguise"—sunglasses, riding boots, slacks, ratty leather jacket, and cigarette holder under a squashed slouch hat —could not understand why people stared. She thought herself invisible in her costume.

"I don't believe you realize how old I am," Cissy confided in a letter to Rose Crabtree. "Really, Ma Reed was a beauty compared to me now—and what's more, she hasn't a doggoned thing on me today for unadulterated meanness."

A scribbler with a talent for self-portraits, Cissy penned one brutal rendering, "T'is I. T'is true, t'is a pity, t'is, t'is Cissy."

14

Death . . .

Cissy's 1943 illness made her aware that it was time to prepare for the deposition of the *Times-Herald* when she was gone. After thirteen years of expending time, energy, and money on the paper, she couldn't conceive of it dying with her. The *Times-Herald* was not the kind of property businessmen wanted to saddle themselves with during the war. Tired and weary of public battles, Cissy would gladly have parted with the paper right then if someone acceptable had taken it off her hands.

She approached brother Joe but he cursorily declined the offer to apply his talents to Washington—a city he had always called a "publishers' graveyard." Cissy then offered to sell the *Times-Herald* to Patterson's daughter, Alicia, who with her husband, Captain Harry Guggenheim, had just launched a little Long Island suburban daily called *Newsday*. But Captain Patterson harshly intervened, "What does Alicia want with a losing newspaper?" he demanded of Cissy. "Stay away from Alicia. You'll only hurt her the way you've hurt everyone else."

With no other acceptable alternatives in sight Cissy offered the *Times-Herald* to her cousin, "Bourbon Bertie," but Colonel McCormick was having none of it. The paper could have been sold to Eugene Meyer, the constant suitor who was eager to merge it out of existence into his *Post*. Cissy, however, insisted that operation of the *Times-Herald* should continue and along with it the anti-internationalist editorial lines she had set since 1941.

Cissy began tinkering with her will to leave the *Times-Herald* to one or more of its executives. Unfortunately—and of course this was the opposite of her intention—this left the paper's management in chaos when she died five years later, thus insuring its demise.

Her interest and energy lagging, Cissy spent less and less time at the *Times-Herald* after 1943. She was rarely seen any more in the city room, which once had so invigorated her with its intrigue and gossip and excitement. She spent her summers at Dower House and Long Island, and her winters in Florida. She scarcely used Fifteen Dupont Circle or her New York apartment, let alone her Nassau property, her Wyoming ranch and her lands in North Dakota.

The *Times-Herald* lurched along, as various editors struggled to interpret Mrs. Patterson's telephone directives. Still, the paper capitalized on the rare journalistic opportunities of the war, when the public was insatiable for battlefront news. In 1943 the *Times-Herald* turned its first modest profit, and in the two succeeding years it earned $610,000 and $897,000. Circulation, the largest in Washington, hovered at 250,000 daily and 300,000 on Sundays.

By 1946, with a new President in the White House and

the paper's staff back from the war, the scene was ripe for the *Times-Herald* to expand and broaden into a first-class newspaper. It was a moneymaker now and its worst organizational hurdles had been overcome. Cissy instructed her staff to establish good relations with the new Chief Executive, Harry S Truman, but in short order the *Times-Herald* was treating him as a poor-imitation Roosevelt. The challenges of the postwar era were more than Cissy could handle.

She tried very hard to get back the zest of the 1938–40 period, but too much had happened and her strength was too low for consistent performance.

Just when she most needed strength, Cissy lost the major inspiration of her life. Joe Patterson died of a liver ailment on May 26, 1946, as he was preparing to attend his fiftieth Groton reunion. The funeral was held at Ossining, New York, in the big house the Captain had covered with camouflage paint thinking it would harmonize with the countryside. His body was then borne to Washington for a military burial in Arlington National Cemetery. On the eve of the final ceremony the chief mourners stayed at Dupont Circle and Cissy, in her desolation, tried again for a reconciliation with Felicia. But it was of no use. "I could just feel love," Felicia remembers. "It frightened me."

The next morning the family gathered outside the mansion to await the procession. Mary King Patterson, the widow, wore simple black, on advice from Cissy that full mourning would be excessive. Then Cissy, the last to appear, swept out, her face obscured by an elaborate veil, her figure clothed in the long black attire of full mourning. Preëmpting the first limousine, meant for the widow,

Cissy rode off after a final tribal command, "We will not cry in public. We mustn't show the white feather."

Shortly after, Evalyn Walsh McLean died. Cissy had kept a vigil all night at Evalyn's deathbed and when, at dawn, Father Walsh performed last rites, Cissy knelt and prayed desperately. Evalyn's unquenchable exuberance was something Cissy could not replace from her own resources.

Following her brother's death, Cissy was appointed co-trustee of the *News* with Colonel McCormick, an arrangement which immediately generated sparks. McCormick actively intervened in the management of the *News*, once Patterson's sole domain, and rarely bothered to consult or advise Cissy. Making matters worse, McCormick vetoed Cissy's suggestion that Patterson's daughter, Alicia, fill the vacancy on the *Tribune* board of directors created by the Captain's death. Cissy felt her niece had proved her newspaper abilities with *Newsday*, and furthermore Cissy was interested in maintaining a strong Patterson contingent in the inner sanctum of the *Tribune*, the original seat of family power. It was the Patterson branch's right to have an additional director, Cissy believed.

Still another point at issue was Cissy's desire that Alicia succeed her as a trustee of the McCormick-Patterson Trust, the legal entity which had been formed to keep control of the *Tribune*, and subsequently the *News*, in the hands of Joseph Medill's blood heirs. In September, 1946, Cissy took the fight to the Colonel's lair, the old Joseph Medill farm at Wheaton, Illinois, now called Cantigny after the First World War battlefield. He would not dare act so arrogantly about the director's seat, Cissy said, if brother Joe was alive. Losing his icy reserve, the Colonel exploded—so memorably that Cissy reminded him of it in a letter a year and a half later. "You were possessed by a queer kind of rage, all out of proportion to the discussion at hand," she wrote. "I won't forget your lunging across the dark verandah at me, gripping the arms of my chair, baring your lower teeth (very odd indeed) and bellowing in my face—'Joe's dead.' "

Their dislike of each other now outbalanced the family loyalty and affection which had been set in childhood and had endured. Cissy slightingly called the crusty mustachioed Colonel and his second wife, Maryland,* "the Royal Family." When the McCormicks visited Dupont Circle in the spring of 1948, Cissy continually quarreled with her cousin, headily reminding him that brother Joe was the only family newspaper genius she recognized. At a cocktail party during the visit Cissy's butler brought in a radio and turned on a speech taped by the Colonel for broadcast over the American Forum of the Air. As Cissy listened to her cousin's voice march on about the Revolution of 1776, her face grew dark. Slamming her hand on the table, she suddenly exclaimed, "My God, get that thing out of here!" Without waiting for a response, she swept from the room and did not reappear for the remainder of the evening.

At the May, 1948, *Tribune* directors' meeting, the argument continued over a seat for Alicia but the impasse remained. To Cissy the Colonel's stubborn refusal was an

* The Colonel's first wife was Amy Adams. When she died in 1937, he gave her a military funeral, which was a rather unusual procedure for a woman. He married Maryland Mathison Hooper in 1941.

attempt to squeeze out the Patterson name from one of the nation's major communications empires. Anxious and resentful, she threatened the Colonel. At a chance meeting in Chicago's Pump Room, Cissy scratched the neck of her cousin, who was sitting in a booth next to hers, and when he turned around, she said chattily: "My God, you just wouldn't believe what an awful day I've had—I've been down at City Hall getting the goods on you." Was she trying to rattle him or was she serious? Cissy thought she knew certain facts about family wills which, if publicized, would weaken or destroy McCormick's power. And she had an idea she could break the Patterson–McCormick trust by withdrawing the ten shares of *Tribune* stock which her Grandfather Medill had left her directly in his will.

Back in Washington, Cissy took a new tack. She composed a letter to the Colonel, informing him that she intended to write a new will leaving most of her *Tribune-News* holdings to Alicia. And she grimly promised that the new will would leave enough liquid assets to pay taxes without forcing Alicia to sell any of her inheritance. Cissy slaved over the eight-page letter, running through fourteen drafts, until it carried the infuriating but casual tone she wanted:

> In the name of God, Bert. Why did you pull that "ham" act at the last directors' meeting in Chicago and, at the stockholders' meeting a few minutes later, go into the same kind of song and dance?
>
> There you stood, putting on your six-foot-four business, waving your arms about, glaring like a maniac, shouting your denunciations of Alicia. Why?

Cissy renewed her threat to reveal irregularities in the family wills, concluding, "I made up my mind if you got tough with me, I'd get tough with you—but good."

Cissy did not post the letter. Among her many notions at the time was that the FBI was monitoring her mail, and she did not want the government in on this quarrel. Instead she dispatched Frank Waldrop to deliver the letter personally to the Colonel at Cantigny. Told that McCormick was not at home, Waldrop went to a roadside phone and called Cissy asking instructions. "He's not really out," she said offhandedly. "He's probably in the bedroom, hiding behind the portieres watching you right now." On the assumption that the Colonel was indeed at home, Waldrop returned and left the explosive letter with a butler.

If McCormick was worried by Cissy's threats, and Mrs. McCormick recalls that her husband was quite agitated, he maintained his composure in public. Not deigning to reply, McCormick took off for Europe, symbolically washing his hands of the affair.

Meanwhile Cissy had engaged a new lawyer, George Bruce Brooks of New York, to revise her will. She no longer felt easy with the family firm in Chicago headed by Weymouth Kirkland, who to her was now strictly a McCormick attorney. She wished to alter her plan to give the *Times-Herald,* tax-free, to a group of the paper's executives. Instead she had decided to leave cash legacies, which would allow the older executives the option of keeping the legacies or applying them toward the purchase of an interest in the paper. Significantly, Cissy considered the new plan a potential opportunity to provide her niece, Alicia, with a major interest in the *Times-*

Herald, thus further strengthening her hand. The stock not bought by the executives would be available for Alicia to purchase, and undoubtedly the available shares would amount to a majority interest. Arranging for a new will was among the few things which held interest for Cissy in the early summer of 1948. The weather in Washington was unbearably hot. And despite a virulent *Times-Herald* campaign, the District of Columbia was disrupting life at Dupont Circle by building a road underpass for Connecticut Avenue. Simultaneously the water pump at Dower House broke down, forcing the servants to carry water from the pond. Life in Washington that spring had become uncivilized, Cissy decided. But she had been to Florida enough that year, she confided to a friend, concluding, "I guess I'm bored."

Seeking a diversion, Cissy went to New York, where at least there was Bruce Brooks to consult. And to brighten the future she made plans to take a private railroad car across the country in August. She wanted to see Mr. Hearst once more and to take one more trip up Wyoming's Cache Creek gorge to Flat Creek and look across at the Tetons.

Back from New York, Cissy immediately found that a Washington rug firm was suing her for $8,200. On the night of July 21 she was served with a subpoena, which she tore up and threw into the officer's face. By July 23, Cissy was back at Dower House. There were neighbors for dinner and one remarked later that Cissy looked especially well, "like a dying tree that sprouts green leaves." Cissy retired early with the prospect of a visit in the morning from her lawyer to discuss the new will. Wearing white beaded pajamas and a cross around her neck, she closed her door at ten-thirty. For reading matter she had the *Times-Herald,* a copy of the draft clause on the revised disposition of the paper, and a novel, *The Golden Violet,* by Joseph Shearing. With her gun in the night-table drawer, her watchdog Butch on the foot of the bed, and a new nightwatchman guarding the house, Cissy began reading Shearing's tale of a lady novelist married for her money and ill-treated by a Jamaican slaveholder, who sought revenge in a love affair with one of the slaves.

Around midnight, as neighbors recall, Butch began barking. The new nightwatchman later said he also heard Butch but didn't investigate and after a while the barking stopped. The next morning Butch straggled into the kitchen as he always did after Cissy let him out of her room. But Cissy did not ring as usual at eight A.M. for breakfast. It seemed a bit unusual but no one chose to disturb the mistress. The servants began their chores except for the gardeners, who waited the signal that Mrs. Patterson had awakened before starting their lawn mowers.

At eleven A.M. Frank Waldrop called from the *Times-Herald* for a telephone editorial conference. Two hours later, he called again, and for the second time he was told that Mrs. Patterson was not up.

Suddenly the butler blurted out, "I think she's dead."

"What do you mean, you *think* she's dead," demanded Waldrop.

"I just think she's dead," came the enigmatic reply.

When Waldrop arrived after the twenty-five-mile drive from Washington, Dower House was in confusion. The cook says she was the first one who looked into the bedroom and saw Cissy slumped over her book, a cigarette burned down to the ashes in her fingers, and her long red hair hanging over the side of her head. A bottle of brandy was on the floor beneath the bed and Madame Bouchard remembers pills scattered about the bedroom.

Six weeks earlier a *Times-Herald* editorial had warned against the dangers of sleep-inducing drugs. "In a world of feminine melodrama," the editorial had cautioned, "sleeping pills can be a many purpose weapon to people of a highly sensitive and emotional turn of mind . . . when they get sick of this whole business of lost husbands, neglected options and fading applause. . . ."

By coincidence, the children of Cissy's second husband, Elmer Schlesinger, dropped in on Dower House that afternoon for a courtesy call. They were part of a large group of friends and neighbors who preceded the doctor to the scene of death. The doctor fixed the time of death at 1:08 A.M., July 24, and wrote the cause as renal disease, a general kidney malfunction.

The funeral was held in the ballroom of Dupont Circle after a public viewing of the casket in the library, where Cissy had been married to Josef Gizycki. Throngs of the curious filed through, attracted by her fame and notoriety. Gaping at the objets d'art and commenting on the rosewood floor, they clogged the room, forming a bottleneck in the hall. The heat was overpowering, so was the odor of some $35,000 worth of flowers, including a casket covering of yellow roses, Cissy's favorite flower. One policeman fainted. So many ashtrays and bibelots disappeared that the force of private detectives had to be doubled. Cissy's ashes were brought back to Chicago for an Episcopalian funeral at St. Chrysostom's Church and buried in the Medill lot at Graceland Cemetery. It was some months before anyone thought to mark her grave with a headstone.

Cousin Bert was in Paris at the time of Cissy's death and did not attend the funeral. When wire service reporters reached him at his hotel, the Colonel said, "This is indeed surprising," adding that it was a "terrible blow." When he hung up the telephone, he began to whistle, absorbed in his own thoughts, and then his wife thought she heard him gently singing the words, "I'm the last leaf upon the tree."*

* From a poem entitled "The Last Leaf" by Oliver Wendell Holmes, Sr. The relevant section reads: "And if I should live to be/ The last leaf upon the tree/ In the spring/ Let them smile, as I do now,/ At the old forsaken bough/ Where I cling."

15

. . . and Taxes

Cissy's death set the town speculating. She had been just about to make a new will and she had hinted she might be murdered. And she had died under odd circumstances, some said. Why had no one investigated her dog's midnight barking? And who had let the dog out of Cissy's room? Drew Pearson told one newspaper; "Before we are through with this, we may find cases of the old circulation skullduggery that was started by the same crowd in Chicago."

Six weeks after Cissy's will was published Charles B. Porter, her financial manager of twenty years, jumped to his death from a hotel room in Clarksburg, West Virginia. Immediately the *Times-Herald*'s top executives sent reporter Sidney Epstein as courier on a chartered private plane to West Virginia to sequester Porter's baggage from his hotel room. The bags contained files on Cissy's life and a diary he had kept about her. In the same week, Betty Hynes, who had begun her career with Cissy as a social secretary and ended as a society reporter, died from an overdose of sleeping pills.

Porter had quit the *Times-Herald* in the spring of 1948 after a humiliating confrontation with Cissy concerning his private life. Still, as one of the executives originally slated to inherit the newspaper, Porter was expecting much from the will and received nothing. His *apparent* suicide, closely followed by Miss Hynes' death, rekindled speculation that he or Cissy or both were murdered. Pearson, echoed by several other voices in the press, kept hinting at foul play. A friend of Porter's told some reporters that Porter had been asked by one of the inheriting executives to support a fraudulent $500,000 claim against the estate. Porter, so the unsupported charge went, refused to knuckle under to threats or to a $50,000 bribe offer.

The controversy over Cissy's will became a scandal when her daughter began legal action to break the testament, claiming that her mother was not of sound mind at her death and had been unduly influenced by certain of her business associates. Cissy had offered Felicia an interest in the *Times-Herald* on more than one occasion, always to be rebuffed. But the newspaper aside, Cissy's bequest to her daughter, her sole legal heir, of a $25,000 annual annuity was not unrestrained largesse for someone leaving a $17,000,000 estate. After an ugly public fight Felicia withdrew her suit and settled for an outright sum of $400,000 in place of the annual income.

Cissy's will hurt a number of people with what appeared little rhyme or reason. Rose Crabtree, Cissy's dearest friend from the Wyoming days, was left little, and Cal Carrington received only an extension in his allowance instead of Cissy's ranch as she had promised. But Evie Roberts, a latter-day friend, inherited a sable wrap, the Youssoupoff black pearls, and valuable business property on Washington's Connecticut Avenue. Betty Hynes was forgotten altogether while Anne Smith received Dower House. Ellen Pearson Arnold, Cissy's only grandchild, was left nothing. The Republican Women's Club of Washington, promised Dupont Circle, saw it go to the Red Cross, and the Tailwaggers Club, an animal clinic founded by Cissy, was left to raise money for itself.

But no one was put in a more tenuous position than the seven executives* who inherited the *Times-Herald*. Three were over sixty years of age and thus professed more interest in cash bequests for their own estate needs than in ownership of the paper. Moreover, Cissy's estate provided few liquid assets to meet the $10,000,000 taxes due. There was virtually no market for her single largest holding, the beneficial units of the McCormick-Patterson Trust. Yet the estate's executors saw no other source for the cash needed to pay taxes and fulfill the other terms of the will than sale of all the units.

To the executives sale of the *Times-Herald* appeared unavoidable and to several of them, desirable. As always Eugene Meyer's *Post* was an eager suitor—so eager that Meyer was willing to buy all unsold units of Cissy's family trust holdings. That threat more than a desire for the *Times-Herald* galvanized Colonel McCormick into action. Within thirteen months of Cissy's death the Tribune

---

* The seven executives named were: William C. Shelton, general manager; Frank C. Waldrop, executive editor; Edmund F. Jewell, advertising director; Michael W. Flynn, managing editor; H. A. Robinson, circulation director; J. Irving Belt, mechanical superintendent; Mason S. Peters, night managing editor. During legal controversies over the will, the press dubbed them "The Seven Dwarfs."

Company was the new owner of the newspaper and of the McCormick-Patterson Trust units which Cissy had hoped to leave in a new will to her niece, Alicia.

In short order McCormick and the Tribune Company returned the *Times-Herald* to a losing property by piling on many of the expenses which Cissy's business managers had systematically stripped away through the years. Under McCormick the *Times-Herald* expanded personnel, added ten news columns daily and seventy on Sundays, enlarged the page size by 10 per cent, increased the number of Sunday sections from four to six, reintroduced financial stock tables, and lowered circulation rates. By 1952 McCormick was losing $80,000 on his new Washington operation. With expenses scheduled to rise another $400,000 in 1953 to $11,834,370, the coming year's operating loss was projected as $557,746.

The Tribune Company's proud boast that it was investing heavily to build future volume was coming a cropper. McCormick appointed as *Times-Herald* editor his niece, Basie, the second daughter of Ruth Hanna and Medill McCormick. But soon the Colonel decided the situation was so grave it demanded his personal on-the-scene attention. Though he came on to Washington and assumed direct control, the paper's fortunes wouldn't snap to attention.

Early in 1954, while the Colonel was at his Florida retreat, an intermediary suggested to Meyer that the *Times-Herald* might finally be for sale. Meyer and his son-in-law, Philip L. Graham, flew to Florida immediately. McCormick, a businessman to the end, cut his losses while professing that he would never have thought of selling the paper if it hadn't been suggested to him by

Kent Cooper, retired general manager of Associated Press and the intermediary who approached Meyer.

For a reported $8,000,000, the *Post,* after so many vain attempts through the years, acquired the *Times-Herald.* With the sale the *Times-Herald* ceased to exist as an independent entity. Washington was left with one morning paper, the *Post* and two afternoons, the *Star* and the *News.* Several of the *Times-Herald*'s executives have questioned their decision since selling to McCormick.

The successful transition of the *Post* and the *Star* into newspapers of great scope and depth suggests that the *Tribune's* long-range estimate of reader demand was correct if its methods hasty. But at the time, with more newspapers competing for the city's smaller advertising dollar, the expensive investment program struck the *Times-Herald* business manager, William Shelton, as a fatal mistake. Shelton's advice to the *Tribune* executives was a neat summary of the eighteen-year era in which Cissy Patterson was an editor and publisher: "I told them you always had to scratch for gains in Washington."

If Colonel McCormick failed with the *Times-Herald,* Captain Patterson's daughter Alicia succeeded without any help from the family. Alicia Patterson, as editor and publisher of *Newsday,* which was owned and managed by her husband, Captain Harry Guggenheim, achieved the most striking success in postwar journalism. When other papers were shrinking, *Newsday* grew with Long Island, won a Pulitzer Prize in 1954, and is today the eighth largest evening paper in the country. Alicia Patterson Guggenheim was just as scrappy as the rest of the family. When her father and her Aunt Cissy were printing statistics to prove that the majority of Americans were isolationists,

Newsday printed a front-page box, "FIGURES DON'T LIE, BUT LIARS SOMETIMES FIGURE." Many people were struck by a similarity between Cissy and Alicia. But Alicia disclaimed it. "I'm not as colorful as Cissy," she said. "I work harder at my job. And I'm loyal to my friends."

With the demise of the *Times-Herald*, Cissy Patterson passed into Washington's folklore. Posters and sawdust were the only tangible remnants of the traveling circus which had been Cissy and her newspaper. The impermanance of her impact on Washington was characteristic of her *après moi, le déluge* career. She had an instinct for accumulating power but not for conserving it. Power leaked out of her hands in driblets of whimsey and revenge, until, at the last, the *Times-Herald* had little influence left.

Cissy's innate sense of direction toward reader interest had made her newspaper the most widely read in the nation's capital. And the *Times-Herald* displayed unusual nerve. It rarely compromised with its opposition, professional or political. To an astounding degree it achieved the independence of which it boasted, detached from the establishment of parties and pressure groups. Washington was kept awake by its virulent competitive spirit, and by its sleuthing.

But for all its assets as a publication—drive, independence, humor, and verve—the paper lacked coherence. It was a newspaper in search of causes, and it latched on to too many flimsy, irrelevant ones. Its readers wearied of hearing about vivisection, allegedly quack doctors, the underpass at Dupont Circle, and the character failings of members of the Roosevelt Administration. The readers became conscious that they were buying poison with their news.

The *Times-Herald,* of course, had been fashioned in Cissy Patterson's image. It wasn't solid, neither was she. It couldn't channel its energies, neither could she. For all its zestfully negative opinions about the Roosevelt Administration, it did not offer reasonable alternatives. The *Times-Herald,* like its mistress, was a gold digger of other people's ideas.

The swings of mood which characterized Cissy and her journalism were caused by too much sail and not enough ballast. She grasped one illusion after another to weight her life, but, like the diamond crucifix she gave Mrs. McLean, they had a way of becoming jokes. Only Cissy's wit cut her bitterness. She was one of the few people who could have tried to jump out of an apartment house window, and, on being restrained by her butler, laugh at the absurdity of the scene.

Cissy's secret, the key to her power over other people and the source of her unhappiness, was her detachment from the rest of humanity. Even in moments of passion or violence a twin Cissy perched outside the situation and made light comments. If Cissy ever gave herself entirely to anything, whether man or child or friend or candidate or God or idea, no record of the transaction remains. Throughout her life in various ways she tried to mitigate her isolation. A female Don Juan, she caused one man after another to swear love, but no number of declarations reassured her. Her friendships with women followed the same pattern. She destroyed human relationships and then mourned them, and she died feeling rejected. When she tried to belong to something outside herself, whether a European aristocracy or a chain of mountains in Wyoming or a newspaper office, she inevitably failed in the attempt. One recalls her sitting in the kitchen of the Crabtree Hotel, pretending to be one of the help, or standing on the threshold of the city room, pretending to be one of the boys.

A perceptive friend remarked on the wistfulness of Cissy's consuming interest in other people's affairs: Cissy was always asking personal questions as if she were seeking a basis of comparison for her own emotions. She thought she was very different from other people and she liked to speculate whether it was her inherited characteristics or her environment which had isolated her. She showed her success by her money, but she also blamed it for her loneliness.

In fact, though one hesitates to name the cause, part of Cissy had been numbed since early childhood, some time between her birth on a windy November morning in Chicago and her secondary schooling on Beacon Street in Boston. Certainly the environment of stone mansions and an estranged family was not a warm one. Cissy's chill went deep, a piece of dry ice stuck in the heart of a passionate woman, steaming and burning as it froze. It baffled people how she could be so warm and so cold at the same time, and too many observers concluded that she lacked feelings. Cissy Patterson was all feelings but no faith—all pain and no remedy. It was symptomatic of a distressing internal malady that she felt imprisoned by her own personality and tried so hard to flee herself.

She discovered one escape early in life—"that release and exhilaration of spirit which comes to very shy people when they appear disguised in fancy dress," as she later put it in a novel. Cissy was an imaginative collector of disguises, literal and figurative. Her library of costumes, from court dress to dog-walking clothes, was exaggeraged enough for the stage, and so were her mannerisms—the grand entrances and gestures, the melodramatic, memorable exits. She had a fascination for false identities. Her reporting adventure at the Salvation Army was not the only incident when she pretended to be someone else.

Yet had she been given the choice, Cissy doubtless would have chosen to be Cissy—a ball of fiery gases whirling through space, fragmentary, held together by velocity, losing sparks and leaving a streak of light in the blackness before she burned out. Few women have enjoyed such power or put themselves through so many emotions. Cissy paid a high price for it. But then she was extravagant.

ABOUT THE AUTHOR

ALICE ALBRIGHT HOGE's mother's family has been publishing and editing newspapers in America for more than a hundred and fifty years. She is the grandniece of Cissy Patterson, and the granddaughter of Captain Joseph Patterson, founder of the New York Daily News; *a descendant of Colonel Robert McCormick, the publisher of the* Chicago Tribune, *and also of Joseph Medill, the patriarch of that newspaper. Mrs. Hoge, red-headed like her Great Aunt Cissy, was born in 1941, graduated in 1962 from Radcliffe College, and was the first woman elected to the editorial board of the* Harvard Crimson. *She is married to James Hoge, city editor of the* Chicago Sun-Times. *They live in a Victorian town house on Chicago's Near North Side, with their three small children.*